Living the Promises

The Lord's Ways
No Longer Mysterious

Written By: Carrie Bertrand

First Page Publications
Livonia, Michigan

First Page Publications
12103 Merriman • Livonia • MI • 48150
1-800-343-3034 • Fax 734-525-4420
www.firstpagepublications.com

Text © 2005 by Carrie Bertrand
All rights reserved

Library of Congress Control Number: 2005905724
Living the Promises/Bertrand, Carrie
ISBN # 1-928623-62-X

Summary: A scripture- and anecdote-based guide to understanding the Bible.

All rights reserved. No part of this publication may be reproduced or transmitted in any form or by any means, electronic or mechanical, including photocopy, recording, or any information storage and retrieval system, without permission in writing from the publisher.

First Page Publications
12103 Merriman Road
Livonia, MI 48150

Acknowledgements

I would like to thank the people who have supported and encouraged me through the writing of this book.

To God my heavenly Father: for the inspiration and continual guidance to fulfill my desire to share his simple but powerful truths.

To my husband Bob: for your love and support, and for always believing in me. For the ability we have to always come together and stand strong as one with God as our foundation and his word for our truth. I love you always.

To my daughter Ashley: for the wonderful person you have become and for being an inspiration to me to continue in God's word. You are a tremendous example to the children, teenagers and adults of this world that God's word is true, and through him there is wisdom far beyond years. I am always proud to call you my daughter and friend.

To Sarah, Brix, Leonard, Julie, Jerry, Tracy, Jackie, Ray, Kurt, and Bonnie: my extreme gratitude to each of you for your time, effort and encouragement, and your part in making this book possible.

May God bless you all.

Introduction

I was one of God's lost sheep and I give my thanks to God, and to his children who introduced me to his word; because of them I am living his promises.

I write this book in hope of doing the same for you. To reveal his word in the intent that God gave it to us. If you are one of his children and you are lost when you come to his word, I believe this book will not only show you what his promises are, but it will introduce God, in a way that he can guide and direct you as his child, when you come to him each day for your personal needs.

In God's word, Jesus gave direction many times through what is referred to as a parable. A parable is simply a similarity or analogy, something we can relate to. In the same respect, I give to you the following. Picture yourself in this position.

Let's say there is a woman you love, but you rarely hear from her when she doesn't have a need. You have been there for her every time she has called on you and every time this happens, she accepts what you gave her saying, "Thank you," and telling you how much she loves you. It's the same routine; you hear from her and she tells you her reasons, or excuses, for how she got into this new mess she is in now. This time she realizes what she has been doing wrong, and she knows how to fix it. If you will give her five thousand dollars, it would clear all her debts and give her a clean slate to start over. She won't need you to keep bailing her out, because she will do a better job this time. You tell her, "I love you and I want to help you, but this is one I'll need to think about. I'll write you tomorrow and let you know."

She receives your nine-page letter that you have put your heart into. On the first page she reads how much you love her, and that you have decided to give her the money. She reads a little further as the letter continues with you telling her of your pride and belief in her, to give her encouragement. In her excitement, because her troubles are over, she sets your letter on the table. She gets sidetracked with phone calls, life and living, and doesn't get back to your letter that explains on page seven, as you wrote, unfortunately you won't have the money until the eighth of the month. You will put the money in a bank account on the ninth. In the closing of your letter on page nine, you tell her the account is in her name, the account number and the name of the bank, and you end your letter saying you love her and God bless.

Months go by, and you have not heard from her, so you call to find out how she's doing. During the conversation, you find that she has been angry with you because she lost everything. Now, her mess is even bigger, and she feels that it's your fault because you didn't give her the money like you said you would. Then she tells you, if you had not told her you would give her the money, she would have found another way.

Like this letter of yours, the analogy is this: The Bible is our letter from our Father written to us telling us of his love, pride, and belief in us, and he tops it off with much encouragement. God tells us in his letter that he gives us what we ask for in this same manner. If we don't care enough to read his letter through page seven to find out when, or page nine to know how to receive what he gave us, do we truly love him, or do we just want what he promised? Are we worthy of what we ask for, if the letter he wrote to us is not important enough that we want to read the whole letter? Also is it his fault if we do not get what he gave us if it's sitting in a bank in our name? Or are we remaining upset with him for what we think are broken promises? Do we know that he ended his letter to us saying, "The grace of our Lord Jesus Christ be with you all. Amen"?

Here is another analogy, for those who receive the letter (the Bible) and cannot read it. If they know God gave them a personal letter of love and promises, and do not want to believe they are idle promises when the first page sounded so encouraging. How long will you allow someone to read the first page over and over to you, before you learn to read the letter yourself?

Isn't it time we learn to read God's word as the personal letter that it was intended to be?

In a simple exciting way, this book will show you God's promises and teach you how to read and understand his letter of love (the Bible) so you can also live his promises.

Preface

Luke 24:45, "Then opened he their understanding, that they might understand the scriptures."[1] God knows that our salvation and our eternal life are mostly dependent on our knowledge and our understanding of his word. He would not have designed it to be any less perfect or detailed than he did the universe or the human body. Think about the details in God's designs, the human body for one. How many things can a doctor know about you, from one drop of your blood? And don't we know the placement of the stars in the year 3000? God did not put less precision in his word, which is the one thing we have to instruct us in him and our hope for salvation. Without his word we could not possibly be sure we know him, and we would have no guidelines established by him. He also would not have designed it to be so complicated that none of us know for sure who is right.

For lack of teaching people how to read, study and understand the Bible for themselves, there are so many people having to accept what they hear and have been taught as if it's the truth from God. This is how we have come to so many different opinions, translations, interpretations and denominations, when we are all reading the same book.

I believe we all want to know God's truth, not just what we choose to believe "because it sounds good." Besides, what if the ones who are teaching us are wrong? And, most of all, how do we know who is right?

This is our eternal life on the line. When it comes to God's word, it does not matter what a friend, relative, minister or denomination says; the only thing that matters is what God said.

God says in the book of 2 Peter 2:1, "There shall be false teachers among you."[2]

James 1:22 says, "Be ye doers of the word and not hearers only, deceiving your own selves."[3]

In John 5:39, Jesus Christ tells you to "search the scriptures, for in them ye think ye have eternal life but they are they which testify of me."[4]

God's word also says in 2 Peter 1:20, "Knowing this first that no prophesy of the scripture is of any private interpretation."[5] These are just a few of God's warnings to us about putting our trust in someone other than him and his word. There are so many people limiting God in their life for lack of teaching or wrong teaching, so this book is written in simple, life-related examples so it will be easy to read, even for those who are not very familiar with the Bible. You will be able to understand it, so that you too can walk with the power that God gave you through Christ.[6] As you read this book you will not only become more familiar with God's word, you will see how his word is directing our lives every day, whether we realize it or not. My prayer is that this book will be an aid in teaching people how to understand God's word as he has said it, so that if you are not already, you will be able to live the more than abundant life God promised you. May God bless you all with great understanding of his wonderful, magnificent word!

Chapter 1
God Gives Us What We Need and Ask For

Since I became a Christian, God has literally shown me signs, miracles and many wonders.[7] He has sent angels on several occasions in my times of need.[8, 9] Once was to tell me what to do at the emergency room to save my husband's life. One drove my car when I fell asleep with the cruise control set. Another saved me from an eighty-foot drop over a waterfall. This was the only one of the three that I did not visually see, but I could feel the hold on my hand, and the next thing I knew, I had a handful of grass that had been several feet away. Also, three other people witnessed this and could not explain it. I wouldn't be surprised if there have been other angels in my life that I didn't recognize as angels. Because God's word says that we entertain angels unawares[10]. But of these three there was no doubt.

I am writing this to you as a true testimony that all of God's wonderful promises are truly available to each of us every day. God did not make his word complicated; we have. Several years ago, God showed me an actual vision that I would like to share with you, along with some history of how this book came about. I was thirty-two years old; I did not know God and I could not even read the Bible. Sure, I had picked it up a few times and tried, but it seemed so confusing to me that I would just put it back down. I was so ignorant of spiritual things that Satan was able to creep in unawares, and he practically destroyed my seemingly perfect little world.[11]

I was so confused that I didn't know what or how this had happened. Since this is not a horror story, I will skip the details for now. The long and short of it is that I told my horror story to Bob, a long-time friend who is also my best friend to this day, and now my husband of nine years. Of all the people who had heard or witnessed the things that had happened to me, he was the first and only one to mention God or Satan. He simply asked me, "Do you know who Jesus Christ is?"[12] and then he proceeded to teach me the word of God. He gave me some details of what the book of Job was about, and he told me to read it. My story was so similar to Job's, right down to the sores from head to toe.[13]

I was so amazed when I read about all the things that happened to Job; the similarities were almost scary. I understood that Job had allowed Satan in by a fear that he harbored for his children.[14] So I looked back at the last two years of my life, analyzing everything that had happened, bringing every detail to the word for explanation, trying to find my fear that had allowed Satan in.[15] Considering the person I was before these things had happened, I was one of the most positive people I knew. I wasn't afraid of anything. When I couldn't recall a fear, I continued searching and found the answers to the whats and the whys of my whole life written in the Bible.

By bringing every thought captive to the word, I saw how it documented every detail. Because of my ignorance of God and Satan and death,[16] I allowed Satan into my home, and from that moment, he continually destroyed my life. My mother-in-law had died recently and, like many people, I had heard all my life different, flippant statements about where she was.[17] At her funeral service, the preacher talked about her being in a better place, and that God had called her home. He also said, "God needed another angel," and this was the one that had allowed Satan into my life. It was easy to believe that if God needed an angel this woman would have been one because she was the most wonderful person I had ever met.

To make a long story short, we bought the house she died in. When we heard her sewing machine running in what used to be her sewing room, I remember talking about this wonderful woman and how she wouldn't harm us. Many things had happened to reveal her presence. We accepted every sign that she was there, and we were not afraid of her. One night, I saw her standing at the foot of our bed, and I softly spoke, "Hi Glendon," and she disappeared into the night.

When I learned later from the Bible that God says when people die they are asleep until Christ comes back,[18] (which hasn't happened yet) I knew that this could not have been Glendon.

God Gives Us What We Need and Ask For

So I continued searching for God's explanation and found that devil spirits can appear in a familiar form.[19] I knew then that because we did not recognize this as an evil spirit, and we did not send it away, in essence we invited what God refers to as a familiar spirit into our home.

When I looked back on what had happened, the day after her appearance was when our life started to be destroyed piece by piece. That piece by piece is a horror story, and would be a book in itself or I wouldn't leave it out. But I, like Job, had allowed a break in the hedge that God told us about in his word.[20]

As I lined up my life with what God's word says, I realized that my whole life could be documented and understood by just the few things I had learned from the Bible. I watched very closely as I began to apply other things from the Bible, and sure enough, like Job my life was put back in order, even better than it was before.

I began to wonder how other people could know God and his word and not have a perfect life.[21] I became so excited for God's word that I started asking God, "What is it that we are all missing? It must be in there; everything else is." I remember thinking, if the Bible is accurate and true, why do so many, even those who know God's word so well, have unresolved issues and problems in their lives? This thought set me on a mission with God and the Bible to find out why, so that I could teach it to others, and we could all live this perfect life that I now believed should be available.[22]

I prayed and prayed, practically pleading with God daily to show it to me.[23] One night, after days of searching the Bible and asking God, I closed the Bible for the night and went to bed.[24] Minutes later, a voice told me to get up. I did not even question it; I got up. I went down the stairs, sat at the table, and I stared at the wall not knowing yet why I was there. It was then that a very large, closed Bible appeared on the wall as clear as a hanging picture, about three feet square. This Bible then opened to the book of Job, and my name was written next to Job's. The pages turned to another book in the Bible, and Bob's name was written next to the name of that book. The pages continued turning in this manner several times, and each book in this Bible had another name of someone I knew written next to the name of the book it had turned to. The last time this happened, the pages turned to the book of Proverbs and there was my name written again next to the word Proverbs. I was totally in awe and I remember thinking, "Okay God, I'm with you, but what does this mean?"

I could hardly contain my excitement; I just knew he was going to show me that one thing—the answer I was looking for that we are all missing. This was the message that I heard: "Carrie, when you came to my word, you found your situation and your answer in my record of Job. You searched my word and found answers throughout it that you could line up with all of your past situations. The answers you seek today are not in Job, but you will find them in my word. There is not any one answer for everyone.[25] Teach my people how to find their daily answers in my word, for the answers they will need each day will be different. Remember always that there is nothing new under the sun; I did not leave any answers out."

Not realizing the degree of this message at that time,[26] what began to sink in was that I realized I must have seemed pretty puffed up to God, thinking that I might find one answer to the world's problems when God himself had to write a whole book of answers. I began to feel really embarrassed, and instantly with that thought, a man's face appeared over the Bible and he winked,[27] saying, "It's okay. I look upon your heart." This was God's reassurance to me that he knew I truly wanted this to help others. Now let me tell you, this was quite an experience.

I began to wonder, did this really happen or did I imagine it? Not feeling sleepy anymore, I opened the Bible to the book of Proverbs and found the answer to the question, did this really happen? Remember God's message? My name was in Proverbs when he ended the first part of his message. When you look for his perfection you will see it. Right there in the book of Proverbs, God said if I lift up my voice and cry after knowledge, he would give it.[24] This is exactly what I had done. Also in Matthew he said that all things whatsoever I shall ask in prayer, believing I shall receive it. According to God's word and his promises, he had to give me what I asked for because I had done what the word says. God himself cannot break his own laws or promises. (He calls them immutable laws.)[28]

It took me years to fully comprehend this message from God, and to mature in God's word enough to know how to use this information to help others. Ten years have passed since this happened. When I was inspired to write this book I debated it, thinking, I am not a writer. God, how can I write a book? And the scripture came to me, "I can do all things through Christ which strengtheneth me."[29] I sat at the table with my Bible, and lo and behold, I read this scripture for the first time in Acts 17:30, "And the times of this ignorance God winked."[27] Once again, years later when I needed this, God reassured me that this really did happen, and that it was meant for me to share the story with others. Also in these same verses were reminders to me of the other things he had said to me that night, that "there is nothing new under the sun."[30]

God had winked at ignorance before, so this was not something new, and the fact that it had been mentioned in his word tells me he really didn't leave anything out. Wow, this seemed like an extensive, detailed message. Looking back now I realize something else. God had shown me an actual vision, like the visions that had been shown to several of his children in the Bible. This confirms that the things that happened to them thousands of years ago really can and do still happen; they are just as available today as they were then.

After considering all this, I thought about what Jesus said to doubting Thomas,[31] "Because you have seen me you have believed, blessed is he who has not seen and yet has believed." Think about this statement from Jesus. What is his message to us? We did not see and talk to Jesus, and we did not see him raised from the dead. And he said, blessed are we who have not seen and yet believe. Believing that God and Jesus meant every word they said is what has allowed me to see God's presence in my life, and this is how I know God did not make idle promises. Thanks to the many people God has sent to reveal his true word to me, God was able to literally show me how perfect his word is, but it saddens me, as I'm sure it saddens God, that so many other people are not seeing it.

This is why I feel the desire to help others to see that signs, miracles and wonders really do follow those who believe. By understanding his word, anyone can have a personal relationship with him.[32] If you walk with God daily, he and his word will direct your path.[33, 34] Learning to read and live by his every word is how to see the depth of everything he gave to you, but more important how to receive them. So you should break down and give considerate thought to everything he said. For example, in 2 Timothy 3:16, the word says, "All scripture is given by inspiration of God and is profitable for doctrine, for reproof and for correction, for instruction in righteousness."[35]

Let's break down this scripture for a better understanding of what we just read. It says God inspired all the scriptures, so all the scriptures came from God (the scriptures are his word). It say's they are profitable to you, for the following: for doctrine, which are the scriptures in the word that tell you the right way of living. Reproof are the scriptures that tell you what you are doing wrong. Correction are the scriptures that will correct it. Instruction are the scriptures that tell you how to be righteous with God. Righteousness are the scriptures that tell you of your righteousness with God. Doesn't this tell you that God said he gives you the answers for your life?

Now that you know what God said his scriptures are for, you should consider why it was told to you in this manner. This will show you how to apply and receive all of them. This is a package deal you have been given. If you don't accept the reproof scriptures you cannot receive the correction because you are not living in all of his truths.[36] Accepting God's truth and living it is what puts you in righteousness. You cannot expect correction if you don't accept and live by his doctrine or reproofs. The truth in them is the only thing that will make you free to receive the correction.

Note again, God said he inspired all scripture. Remember everything he has done is as perfect as the universe and the stars, so never give authority to anything that is not documented by his scriptures. God will direct your path and he would not have left anything out of his word that you or he would need in order for him to do this.

Have you ever said, why did God allow this to happen? If so, then is it possible that Satan has blinded you to the light of God's glorious gospel? The scriptures tell us there is confusion in every evil work.[37] Would you ask this question if you were not confused? The world and everything that happens in it can be explained by God's written word.[38] In James we are informed that there is also a wisdom available that comes from above.[39] It also says in 1 Corinthians that there is a wisdom that comes not in words that man's wisdom teaches.[40-44] So what is this wisdom that man cannot teach us? It is wisdom beyond what books or man can give you; it is where the depth of understanding comes from. Through God and his word, all things can be understood and corrected by his instruction. Take a second to re-read 2 Timothy 3:16, and consider every word.

God said, "Ye have forgotten me and trusted in falsehoods."[45] You could be trusting falsehoods if you trust anything you hear that you have not confirmed from God and his word. To confirm and avoid falsehoods, he said to bring every thought into captivity to the obedience of Christ. The word "captivity" means to bring captive and hold on to it; this is what we need to do with God's word. So, the first thing we need to know is Christ's obedience.[15]

Most of us have heard the phrase, "What would Jesus do?" Jesus said many times, "It is written." So we know he knew the scriptures; that's why he said, "I do the will of my Father."[46] We are to follow his examples. So we know we are to do the will of the Father, which is written in all the scriptures; we also know he said God inspired all of them.

It is documented many times in the word that Jesus talked to his Father and followed his Father's direction. He even said, "Let thy will be done and not mine,"[47] and he also said, "I speak not of myself but of my Father which sent me."[48] If we are not talking to God and listening, he cannot give us his answers. If we do not know his scriptures, are we not directing our own path? Doing his Father's will is one thing we know for sure Jesus always did. If we follow this example from Jesus, we can also find these answers that can only come from above.

Looking to God and his scriptures for direction in everything we think and do is the way to acknowledge him so he can direct our path. This is what Christ did. When things happen in our lives, we are to search God, his word and his scriptures to find the answers. God's scriptures tell us to hide his word in our heart.[49] Is this a beating heart he is referring to? How can you hide his word in that? You should consider, if you haven't already, if the heart he was referring to was literal. The heart is the innermost part of you. Your desires and your reasons for what you do are what make you, you. The heart is also what God said he looks upon.[50] Why would he use this analogy? What could he think about you? Yep, it's still beating. The heart is something without which you cannot survive. His word is perfect and as deep as we want to see it. It is easier to walk with God directing our paths than many people realize.

One example of this was when I recently had to make some important decisions, and I talked to God about them the same way Jesus did. I immediately knew what to do and followed through with the first things that came to me. As I was following through with the laid-out plan a few days later, I started to second-guess my decisions, wondering, am I doing the right thing? My next thought was, trust in me for I am with you. I smiled and thanked God for the reassurance, and was able to continue my tasks with full confidence, faith and trust. This is how easily God directs our paths when we allow him to. We can communicate with God the same way Jesus Christ did. If we listen, he will answer and direct us the same way, but there may be times when we must also be willing to say, "Let your will be done and not mine."

God's word is real. This wisdom that is available can only come from above, but it has been kept hidden from so many. It was made available to each of God's children, but how can we receive something that we do not know is available? This is what God said to us in James 3:17, "But the wisdom that is from above is first pure, then peaceable, gentle, and easy to be entreated, full of mercy and good fruits, without partiality, and without hypocrisy."[39]

In the book of Daniel, which was written for our learning, there is an account of a messenger who came to Daniel and said, "Fear not Daniel: for from the first day that you did set your heart to understand and to humble yourself before your God, your words were heard, and I am come for your words."[51] Then the messenger said to Daniel, "I will show you that which is noted in the scriptures."[52] The message to us is that if we set our heart to understand and humble ourselves to God, when we need answers, God will give them and show them to us, even if he has to send a messenger or an angel. For the Bible says, Trust in the Lord with all your heart, lean not unto your own understanding, in all your ways acknowledge him and he shall direct your paths.[33, 34] This is part of how we live by every word that proceeds out of the mouth of God. The Bible said God is not a man that he should lie, and that he is no respecter of persons. If he would give this to Daniel, he would certainly give it to us if we learn how to claim it.

Once you have heard God's answers, or you have read the scriptures and are sure God has said something, hold them captive and don't let any other thought or person confuse you or contradict what he has said. Any doubt, contradiction or confusion usually comes from Satan. We know this because God's word says Satan is the thief, and he comes to steal, to kill and to destroy.[53] The first thing he will try to steal from you is the word of God, because understanding it is your power to defeat him. Walk with confidence and trust that God will never contradict himself in his word or change your direction midstream. That would make him no more perfect than man. God said what he meant and he meant what he said. The word says God is not the author of confusion and that every evil work comes from Satan. Hold captive the understanding that when negative things happen or confusion comes in,[16] God did not allow it, we did, so we just need to get wise to Satan's devices so he no longer has the advantage.

With all this in mind, one very important point I would like to make is this: when you pray to God, end your prayer in the name of Jesus Christ. This is one of your main key ingredients to receiving from God because the Bible says, "That at the name of Jesus Christ, every knee shall bow,"[54] and it also says, "There is one mediator between God and man, that is the man Christ Jesus."[55] God's word says several times in many different ways, he will give you whatsoever you shall ask in the name of Jesus Christ.[56]

You may even want to pray or simply thank God for your understanding and being enlightened, before you continue reading this book. This will rebuke Satan from your path so that Satan cannot blind your mind to the light of God's glorious gospel.

Follow the Bible, not just any man, to find God's word. People can guide and direct you, but only one man (Christ Jesus) can save you. God has designed his word with awesome perfection and simplicity for us to live by. Man has complicated the Bible, not God. My life has drastically changed since I learned God's wonderful word. Read the following scriptures and answer, are you living the promises?

> 1 Timothy 4:12, ". . . but be thou an example of the believers, in word, in conversation, in charity, in spirit, in faith, in purity."

Are you a living example of the word of God that you know?

> 3 John 2:2 "Beloved, I wish above all things that thou mayest prosper and be in health, even as thy soul prospereth."

Are you prospering and in health?

> Hebrews 2:4: "God also bearing them witness, both with signs and wonders, and with divers miracles, and gifts of the Holy Ghost, according to his own will."

Do signs, miracles and wonders follow you wherever you go?

> Matthew 7:8: "For every one that asketh receiveth; and he that seeketh findeth; and to him that knocketh it shall be opened."

Are you receiving all that you ask for?

> Malachi 3:10: "Bring ye all the tithes into the storehouse, that there may be meat in mine house, and prove me now herewith, saith the Lord of hosts, if I will not open you the windows of heaven, and pour you out a blessing, that there shall not be room enough to receive it."

Are the windows of heaven pouring out blessings so that you cannot possibly receive it all?

> 1 Timothy 4:15 "Meditate upon these things; give thyself wholly to them; that thy profiting may appear to all."

Does your profiting appear unto all?

John 14:12 "Verily, verily, I say unto you, he that believeth on me, the works that I do shall he do also; and greater works than these shall he do; because I go unto my Father."

Are you doing all the things that Jesus Christ did?

Do you know what the greater things are?

These are just a few of the scriptural promises God says you should have as his dear children.

Do you believe the promises from God and Jesus Christ are literal?

If you answered no to any of these questions, then ask yourself, do you want to be an example of these promises and their truth? Or do you just want to believe in the possibility that they exist?

Each of the following Bible scriptures are God's word written to us, with reference to where they were used in chapter one. They all document that these things I have experienced and I have written are not only possible but also available. Studying them and searching them and lining them up with your life is how you can make his word your own.

If you use God's word every day and in every situation, your life and your understanding will change.[57, 58] The more you use God's word to document your life and your decisions, the quicker you will see results in your life. If you are not seeing the desired results, God said, "Seek and ye shall find." God's word is perfect; if used correctly you can expect perfect results.

At times where a message is written directly to you in the Bible, the old English was used—thou, thy, or thine; for easier reading of the personal messages, I have used our familiar English, "thou" is you "thy" is the person of reference, "thine" is your.

Chapters throughout this book will be followed by a list of scriptures. If you wish to study them they are according to the King James Version. I have also chosen to follow that same example for capitalization, etc. for this entire book. Notice how many scriptures are used in the chapters because of how often the Bible is referred to and documented in each chapter.[57] Using more than one verse to document a situation for daily decisions and understanding in life and living, is how we are bringing every thought captive to the word.[58]

This format also shows you the exactness of the Bible in our daily life.

Scriptures, Preface and Chapter 1

1. **Luke 24:45** Then opened he their understanding, that they might understand the scriptures . . .
2. **2 Peter 2:1** . . . even as there shall be false teachers among you, who privily shall bring in damnable heresies, even denying the Lord that bought them . . .
3. **James 1:22** But be ye doers of the word, and not hearers only, deceiving your own selves.
4. **John 5:39** Search the scriptures; for in them ye think ye have eternal life; and they are they which testify of me.
5. **2 Peter 1:20** Knowing this first that no prophesy of the scripture is of any private interpretation.
6. **1 John 5:20** . . . the Son of God is come, and hath given us an understanding . . .
7. **Hebrews 2:4** God also bearing *them* witness, both with signs and wonders, and with divers miracles, and gifts of the Holy Ghost, according to his own will.
8. **Revelations 22:6** . . . the Lord God of the holy prophets sent his angel to shew unto his servants the things which must shortly be done.
9. **Matthew 4:11** Then the devil leaveth him, and, behold, angels came and ministered unto him.
10. **Hebrews 13:2** . . . thereby some have entertained angels unawares . . .
11. **Psalms 35:8** Let destruction come upon him at unawares.
12. **2 Timothy 2:24** . . . but be gentle unto all *men,* apt to teach, patient.

13. **Job 2:7** So went Satan forth from the presence of the Lord, and smote Job with sore boils from the sole of his foot unto his crown.
14. **Job 1:5** . . . for Job said, It may be that my sons have sinned, and cursed God in their hearts. Thus did Job continually.
15. **2 Corinthians 10:5** . . . bringing into captivity every thought to the obedience of Christ . . .
16. **2 Corinthians 2:11** Lest Satan should get an advantage of us: for we are not ignorant of his devices.
17. **1 Thessalonians 4:13** But I would not have you to be ignorant, brethren, concerning them which are asleep.
18. **1 Thessalonians 4:14** For if we believe that Jesus died and rose again, even so them also which sleep in Jesus will God bring with him.
19. **Leviticus 19:31** Regard not them that have familiar spirits, neither seek after wizards, to be defiled by them: I *am* the Lord your God.
20. **Job 1:10** Hast not thou made an hedge about him . . .
21. **Proverbs 21:2** Every way of a man *is* right in his own eyes; but the Lord pondereth the hearts . . .
22. **2 Timothy 3:17** That the man of God may be perfect, throughly furnished unto all good works.
23. **Proverbs 2:2** So that thou incline thine ear unto wisdom, *and* apply thine heart to understanding . . .
24. **Proverbs 2:3** Yea, if thou criest after knowledge, *and* liftest up thy voice for understanding . . .
25. **Proverbs 2:5** Then shalt thou understand the fear of the Lord, and find the knowledge of God.
26. **Matthew 21:22** And all things, whatsoever ye shall ask in prayer, believing, ye shall receive.
27. **Acts 17:30** And the times of this ignorance God winked at; now commandeth all men every where to repent . . .

28. **Hebrews 6:18** That by two immutable things, in which *it* was impossible for God to lie . . .
29. **Philippians 4:13** I can do all things through Christ which strengtheneth me.
30. **Ecclesiastes 1:9** The thing that hath been, it *is* that which shall be; and that which *is* done *is* that which shall be done: and there is no new thing under the sun.
31. **John 20:29** Jesus saith unto him, Thomas, because thou hast seen me, thou hast believed: blessed *are* they that have not seen, and *yet* have believed.
32. **2 Corinthians 4:4** . . . the god of this world hath blinded the minds of them which believe not, lest the light of the glorious gospel of Christ, who is the image of God, should shine unto them.
33. **Proverbs 3:5** Trust in the Lord with all thine your heart, and lean not unto thine own understanding.
34. **Proverbs 3:6** In all thy ways acknowledge him, and he shall direct thy paths.
35. **2 Timothy 3:16** All scripture *is* given by inspiration of God, and *is* profitable for doctrine, for reproof, for correction, for instruction in righteousness . . .
36. **2 Timothy 2:15** Study to shew yourself approved unto God, a workman that needeth not to be ashamed rightly dividing the word of truth.
37. **James 3:16** . . . there *is* confusion and every evil work.
38. **2 Corinthians 10:5** Casting down imaginations, and every high thing that exalteth itself against the knowledge of God, and bringing into captivity every thought to the obedience of Christ.
39. **James 3:17** But the wisdom that is from above is first pure, then peaceable, gentle, *and* easy to be entreated, full of mercy and good fruits, without partiality, and without hypocrisy.
40. **1 Corinthians 3:19** For the wisdom of this world is foolishness with God . . .

41. **1 Corinthians 2:14** But the natural man receiveth not the things of the spirit of God: for they are foolishness unto him . . .
42. **1 Corinthians 2:7** But we speak the wisdom of God in a mystery, *even* the hidden *wisdom*, which God ordained before the world unto our glory.
43. **1 Corinthians 2:13** . . . not in the words which man's wisdom teacheth, but which the Holy Ghost teacheth . . .
44. **1 Corinthians 2:6** . . . yet not the wisdom of this world, nor of the princes of this world, that come to naught.
45. **Jeremiah 13:25** This *is* thy lot, the portion of thy measures from me, saith the Lord; because thou hast forgotten me, and trusted in falsehood.
46. **John 6:38** . . . not to do my own will, but the will of him that sent me.
47. **Matthew 26:39** . . . not as I will, but as thou will.
48. **John 12:49** For I have not spoken of myself, but the Father which sent me, he gave me a commandment, what I should say, and what I should speak.
49. **Job 22:22** . . . lay up his words in thine heart. Also see Psalms 119:11.
50. **Proverbs 21:2** Every man *is* right in his own eyes: but the Lord pondereth the hearts . . .
51. **Daniel 10:12** . . . fear not, Daniel: for from the first day that thou didst set thine heart to understand, and to chasten thy self before thy God, thy words were heard, and I am come for thy words.
52. **Daniel 10:21** But I will shew thee that which is noted in the scripture of truth . . .
53. **John 10:10** The thief cometh not, but for to steal, and to kill, and to destroy . . .
54. **Philippians 2:10** That at the name of Jesus every knee should bow . . .

55. **1 Timothy 2:5** For *there is* one God, and one mediator between God and men, the man Christ Jesus.

56. **John 14:13** And whatsoever ye shall ask in my name, that will I do, that the Father may be glorified in the Son.

57. **Matthew 4:4** . . . It is written, Man shall not live by bread alone, but by every word that proceedeth out of the mouth of God.

58. **Ephesians 1:18** The eyes of your understanding being enlightened . . .

Chapter 2
God Won't Let Us Down When We Believe and Trust Him

Almost fourteen years ago, before I knew God and his word, I still managed to have a great life. I thought I had it all: great marriage, beautiful home and I owned my own business for ten years with a secretary and thirty-two employees. This was about the time my life started turning upside down. It seemed like anything bad that could happen, happened. I was pregnant with my daughter and was not quite into the fifth month. I was overjoyed with having my first child at nearly thirty. I went to work one morning and by noon I was feeling a slight tightening in my abdomen, so I went home and called my doctor. He said he would meet me at the emergency room and I asked, "Why? It just feels like I have done too many sit-ups." I had no idea what was going on. I soon found out that these were contractions, and by the time I got to the hospital, they were four minutes apart. I went through the rest of the pregnancy literally on the couch, with a home nurse, self-administered shots and an IV to boot.

Looking back on that situation, no matter what had happened, I was continually positive and confident for my baby. I knew she would be fine, and my every thought was that she would be strong and healthy. She was born premature, but in the recovery room, as she lay on my chest, she actually lifted her head and looked into my eyes. She was released from the hospital less than fifteen hours after she was born. This was one of the situations I searched when I first learned God's word because I wanted to understand why everything else in my life was lost, and she wasn't. I also wanted to understand why my outcome with her was so perfect when others in similar situations are less fortunate.

I know beyond a shadow of a doubt that this was not because I was lucky, only in that area. It was God and positive believing because I received exactly what I had believed for. Ashley was amazingly strong as an infant and to this day I thank God continually for her health and strength. Her strength has not just been physical; she has such a strong positive mind and disposition that she amazes me.

God means what he says; we receive "exceeding abundantly above all that we ask or think."[1, 2]

God's word shows us several examples that what we believe in our hearts will be exactly what we get. His account of Samson and Delilah is one of those great examples. For those who are not familiar with this account, it is located in the book of Judges, chapters fifteen and sixteen. Samson was a man of God and this is mentioned several times through this account because the story tells us the spirit of the Lord came mightily upon him.[3] Samson was a man of great strength and he loved a woman named Delilah, and it says that he told her all his heart.[4] So this was his heart's belief that if he be shaven, his strength would go from him, because he said, "I shall become weak . . ." So even though Samson knew God, his believing was that his hair was his strength. While Sampson slept, Delilah called for a man. She had this man shave off the seven locks of his head.[5] Then it says, "his strength went from him." God did not leave Samson because of a hair cut, and hair does not make a person strong.

When Samson's hair grew back, he then believed he had his strength back. But, the first thing Samson did when his hair did grow back was to call unto the Lord, and he said, "O Lord God, remember me, I pray thee, and strengthen me."[6] God did not turn away from Samson; Samson had turned away from God. This is why he asked God if he remembered him; he obviously hadn't talked to God in a while.

Samson had his strength back because of his believing. We all do this same thing. We set our believing in ourselves and other things for our strength and abilities, and walk away from God like Samson did. The greatest part of this message, for us in this example, is that the first time Samson called to the Lord God, he immediately received what he asked for. It is obvious that his believing had limited him to what he already had. Samson didn't work out and lift weights; his strength was in the Lord, not his hair or muscles.[7] The same is true for us.

Many of us have heard the saying that the Lord works in mysterious ways, but the accounts in the Bible are examples to use in our own lives to help clear the mysteries, if we understand the message. I have seen and believe God's promises, and believe that his word is truth.[8] These details are directing our lives and our situations, like Samson, whether we realize it or not.[9] The moment we stop trying to do things according to our own beliefs and abilities is the moment God gives what we ask. Our son, Aaron, is great proof of what God can and will do the moment we allow him to.

I had always wanted at least two children. After all the trouble I had carrying Ashley to term, I had fear and lacked in my believing. The doctors added to and confirmed every fear that I had. As hard as I tried, I could not get over them for some reason, and I knew even God could not make this happen because of my doubts and fears. In four years we went through six miscarriages, and in every pregnancy I made it to about the fourth or fifth month. The last one was triplets and I lost one in the third month, one in the fourth month and the last one we lost near to the fifth month. After everything we had been through, my family and I agreed that God must have a different plan, and God knows best, so we decided to stop trying to do this our way. We prayed together, simply thanked God for his will to be done, and we didn't dwell on it.

On January 11, I received a phone call from Bonnie, a woman who had been working for us for a long time. She was aware of our many unsuccessful attempts at having a baby, and she knew what a great sadness this was for us. When she called that day, she said she knew a young woman that was in her seventh month of pregnancy who had been planning and preparing to give the baby up for adoption to a good family. Bonnie had told her our story. She was touched and wanted to meet us, and she wanted to know if we would be interested in adoption. I called Bob, and within thirty minutes we met at the house and drove to meet her. If there has ever been a God-sent gift, this was one of them. This woman was wonderful, and she was a very special person. Everything about the situation was as perfect as her admirable reasons for the choices she had made. This had not been easy for her, but she was incredibly strong about the well-being of the baby. God's presence and direction was so evident in the perfection of every detail. Aaron was handed to me in the delivery room on March 9, the same week our last miscarried child would have been born. We brought him home from the hospital with a fully completed adoption, including the home study and our name on the birth certificate. You talk about signs, miracles and wonders; let me tell you, they were continual for those two months. Even the biological father shook our hand and congratulated us on our beautiful son as he left the hospital that day.

There were so many wonderful things that God had done to bring this together so perfectly, but the point of this is to show people that God and his word are not mysterious, they are perfect. God has given us his word and he also said he would not lie. Our Father does as much or as little for us as we allow him to do. Sometimes we just need to step out of the way, let go and let God.

You know each and every one of us has our stories from our life experiences. Whether God and his wonderful word are a part of your daily life is totally up to you; no person has the right to choose for you or condemn you either way for your choices. But what I have found that I want to share with others is that perfect peace and inner joy in my life when I have chosen to allow God to direct my life. We have to choose, in every situation in our lives, to hand them over to God. Sure, we still have opportunities because we are human. We make our own choices and we do have an adversary (the devil), but God has proven his matchless word over and over in our lives and in our daily situations.

Happiness comes from the outside. When things are going well and when people have fun things going on in life, they are happy. But when trouble comes, the happiness goes. But God gives his children something he calls the fruit of the spirit, and through this, we can have an inner joy that never goes, even when trouble comes. This fruit of the spirit that God promised is love, joy, peace, longsuffering, gentleness, goodness, faith, meekness, and temperance.[10] Against such God said there is no law.[11] There is an inner peace that comes from having an understanding of the whats and whys in life. Trust me; things do not happen by luck or chance. To truly love God is to know and understand him and his word.

My reasons for sharing my life experiences with you are simply to show, by example, how to recognize and apply God's word in your daily situations.[12, 13]

Scriptures, Chapter 2

1. **Ephesians 3:20** Now unto him that is able to do exceeding abundantly above all that we ask or think, according to the power that worketh in us . . .
2. **John 10:10** . . . I am come that they might have life, and that they might have *it* more abundantly.
3. **Judges 15:14** . . . the Spirit of the Lord came mightily upon him, and the cords that *were* upon his arms became as flax that was burnt with fire, and his bands loosed from off his hands.
4. **Judges 16:17** That he told her all his heart . . . if I be shaven, then my strength will go from me, and I shall become weak . . .
5. **Judges 16:19** And she made him sleep upon her knees; and she called for a man, and she caused him to shave off the seven locks of his head . . .
6. **Judges 16:28** And Sampson called unto the Lord, and said, O Lord God, remember me, I pray thee, and strengtheneth me . . .
7. **1 Timothy 4:8** For bodily exercise profiteth little . . .
8. **Ephesians 1:13** In whom ye also *trusted*, after that ye heard the word of truth, the gospel of your salvation: in whom also after that ye believed, ye were sealed with that holy Spirit of promise.
9. **Ephesians 1:11** In whom also we have obtained an inheritance, being predestinated according to the purpose of him who worketh all things after the counsel of his own will . . .
10. **Galatians 5:22** But the fruit of the Spirit is love, joy, peace, longsuffering, gentleness, goodness, faith.
11. **Galatians 5:23** Meekness, temperance: against such there is no law.
12. **Matthew 11:15** He that hath ears to hear, let him hear.
13. **Jeremiah 13:15** Hear ye, and give ear; be not proud; for the Lord hath spoken.

Chapter 3
Whose Truth Are We Searching For?

Now ask yourself, do you really want to know God's truth?

John 8:32 says, "And ye shall know the truth, and the truth shall make you free."[1] I ask this question because it's very important to make this decision, knowing up front that the truth may not always be what you want to hear. Because God's word is not of any denomination or religion, some of the things you will learn as you read and study may go against what you have been taught or believed all your life. Change is not always easy, but it is God's truth that makes you free; not mine, not yours or your church's.

Are you willing to change your thinking if God's word shows you that you have been wrongly taught? This is why I ask, do you really want to live by every word that proceeds out of the mouth of God,[2] or do you want religion? We are not learning a religion, we are learning God's word so we can receive the full benefits, seeing those signs and miracles[3] and talking to angels,[4] living the more-than-abundant life of unlimited results.[5, 6] Isn't this our desire and what we are searching for?

If we are truly Christians who seek to follow what God says then it should not matter what a denomination, friend or a relative says; all that should matter to you is what God says. Religions are separating Christians from each other, and in some cases, they are doing more damage than good by all the double talk and flippant statements that confuse and limit people with God. Preachers, teachers and churches can't even agree on the Bible, so why should the common man or woman? This is also causing many people to lose the desire to hear God's word and some even to avoid church. In many cases, it's only the religion they are avoiding, like it's a disease, and who can blame them? Let me give you a few examples of the statements we often hear that are limiting us with God and causing destruction. I'm sure most of you have heard these statements at least once in your lives, and they all contradict God's word. Some of us may have even said them ourselves, because it's what we have been taught. Have you ever heard or said, "God will not give you more than you can handle." Maybe this one: "God is punishing me."[7] If what you are handling are negatives, then you are not getting them from God. There is a common misunderstanding of this verse in the Bible. 1 Corinthians 10:13 says, "God is faithful, who will not suffer you to be tempted above that ye are able; but will with the temptation also make a way to escape, that ye may be able to bear it." The context was concerning people from the time of Moses, who were used as examples from the Old Testament. It specifically states that they were destroyed of serpents in verse 9. In verse 10 it says they were destroyed of the destroyer. God is neither serpent nor destroyer. Now read the first part of the same verse. 1 Corinthians 10:13, "There hath no temptation taken you but such as is common to man." The example for us here is that if we are tempted like they were, by the serpent, God will make ways for us to escape. What about these statements we hear when a person dies: "He is in a better place," or "It was her time," or "God needed another angel." These are commonly said to give us comfort, but the Bible says that death comes from Satan.[8-10] So every one of these statements contradicts what God's word really says. If you think about these statements and try to line them up with God's promises, you might understand why so many people in this world are not walking in power but instead are walking in defeat.

These untruths are causing more harm than we realize. How can anyone believe in God for confidence and power when we hear all these negative untruths about him all the time? Doesn't this show us how the world is twisting God's word?

God has said for us to "be likeminded one toward another according to Christ Jesus."[11] We are reading the same Bible, so I can't help but ask this question: why do we have so many different denominations and religions? There can only be one truth. Are we searching for the truth according to Carrie or the truth according to the right Reverend so-and-so or are we searching for God's truth?

The only way to have one truth is for us to be likeminded to the word and what it says. I am not against any denomination or religion, but I am against statements or teachings that go against God's word and his truth. Especially when it has limited so many of the people I meet, and I myself was one of them.

All through the word of God, the only names for us that God mentions in reference to believers is Christian,[12] which means "Christ in you" or saints who are in Christ Jesus. Understanding what Christ in you means, and the power it gives you, is a critical piece of information, in order for you to know for sure who you are in Christ.[13] If your understanding is limited, your life may not be as fruitful. It is important to have a church or support group; just be cautious of what you are being taught. You are God's child and you can go directly to him every second of every day through Jesus Christ. The word says there is one mediator between God and man, and that is the man Christ Jesus.[14] Think for a moment, what is a mediator? A mediator is someone who communicates and delivers messages back and forth. This is what Christ does for you. So no matter where you go to church, never let anyone take away your personal, immediate connection with your Father through his Son.

It does not matter who said it; if what they say goes against the truth, then it is a lie, and this is when it becomes a person's or a religion's opinion.[15]

This world has become so caught up on religion and politics that we are accepting less than the whole truth because of who said it or because most of what was said sounded good. I want it all, don't you? The whole truth and nothing but the truth, so help us God. When we attend any church we deserve, as God's children, to know that his word is what we are hearing. And how do we know if we do not, or cannot, go home and study?[16] This book is not written about religion and politics. It is written to help people understand the Bible for themselves and to enable them to see the deeper truths that Satan is blinding our eyes to.[17] Don't we all want to walk in the light of this glorious gospel we are hearing about? I pray that this doesn't offend people, but it's all of the truth that makes us free, not just the things that don't offend us. Again, it is not my truth God wants us to find, it's his, and that should be what we all want to stand on. As it says in Isaiah 43:27, "Thy first fathers hath sinned, and thy teachers have transgressed against me."[18] Maybe the teachers have been so focused on teaching what they have heard or have been taught, that many have transgressed against God and have forgotten to be workmen of the word. And have forgotten that they are teachers instead of preachers when we go before them to learn. Or maybe they have not been honest or confident enough to teach the whole truth, because they might offend someone or have to change their traditions or beliefs.

If you are one of God's children who have been wrongly taught, some of the truths that are revealed from God's word may seem, on the surface, to be offensive to some. So I remind you that God said in his word that the truth shall make you free.

When you accept the truth in your heart, God says, "your understanding will be enlightened."[19] And in Ephesians 1:17, "That the God of our Lord Jesus Christ, the Father of Glory, may give unto you the spirit of wisdom and revelation in the knowledge of him."[20] This means the way you see, hear and understand things will change your life, and quite possibly your religion, or even your friends. If you do not have abundance and confidence in your understanding of the word of God, then something or someone is holding you back. I feel a need to make a point that the truth may not always be what you want to hear, because you may have to change when you accept it, and change is not always easy. If you have been following wrong teachings, or the doctrines of men, the second you accept the truth, you can be assured that God forgives you, because it says in Luke 15:7 that "likewise joy shall be in heaven over one sinner that repenteth," (repent means change of mind and accept the truth).[21] The word also says that we should "teach in meekness, instructing those that oppose themselves; and to the acknowledging of the truth; that they may recover themselves out of the snare of the devil, which are taken captive by him at his will."[22, 23] Is it possible that people are being taken captive at the devil's will, for lack of truth or instruction from the teachers? To correct this, believe nothing but God's word as truth, no matter who says it.

One of the first things you need to know and understand is how to distinguish truth from error when God's word is spoken or taught.

God warned us of false teachers on many occasions throughout his word,[24] so first and foremost, understand it and learn to walk only in God's truth.

One way to do this is to read his every word for comprehension. Once you know what God said, do not ever let anyone or anything contradict it. If he said that he does not tempt and neither can he be tempted, don't let anyone tell you God is testing or tempting you. Have you heard the old cliché that God will not give you more than you can handle? God's word didn't say that to mean God would tempt or test us with negatives; that contradicts what he said in James 1:13, "God cannot tempt neither tempteth he any man."[7] So blame the true culprit. If you are hit with troubles or negatives, they are fiery darts,[25] and they are from Satan. Don't let people blame our Father who says, "Beloved I wish above all things that thou mayest prosper and be in health, even as thy soul prospereth."[26] This is God's truth. He also said, "I will never leave thee nor forsake thee."[27] Things you hear and are taught through sermons and things people flippantly say that contradict any of God's scriptures are untruths. God never contradicts his own word, only man does. We must study to determine truth from error.

Life is tough enough as it is, but when we search for answers and everyone has a different one, how do we get results and know who to listen to? Because of untrue answers and statements, my life was practically destroyed and I was left helpless, desperate, in despair, and wondering, why me God? What did I do? How do I fix it or do I give up? Well, in all my searching, I found those answers and many more. The ways of the Lord are not mysterious when you understand him.

When I first started writing this book, I talked to God because some of the things in this book seem bold and harsh, and I debated with God about it. And God simply said to me, "People need to hear the truth; it's time. Those who have ears to hear will hear."[28]

Are you sure you want to know the truth? God said in 3 John 1:4 that he has no greater joy than to hear that his children walk in truth.[29]

Scriptures, Chapter 3

1. **John 8:32** And ye shall know the truth, and the truth shall make you free.
2. **Matthew 4:4** But he answered and said, it is written, man shall not live by bread alone, but by every word that proceedeth out of the mouth of God.
3. **Hebrews 2:4** God also bearing them witness, both with signs and wonders, and with divers miracles, and gifts of the Holy Ghost, according to his own will?
4. **Mark 16:17** And these signs shall follow them that believe . . .
5. **John 1:51** . . . Hereafter ye shall see heaven open, and the angels of God ascending and descending upon the Son of man.
6. **John 10:10** . . . I am come that they might have life, and that they might have *it* more abundantly.
7. **James 1:13** Let no man say when he is tempted, I am tempted of God: for God cannot be tempted with evil, neither tempteth he any man . . .
8. **Hebrews 2:14** . . . that had the power of death, *that* is the Devil.
9. **1 Corinthians 15:26** The last enemy that shall be destroyed is death.
10. **1 Corinthians 15:54** . . . Death is swallowed up in victory.
11. **Romans 15:5** . . . grant you to be likeminded one toward another according to Christ Jesus.
12. **Acts 11:26** . . . and taught much people. And the disciples were called Christians first in Antioch.
13. **Ephesians 1:19** And what *is* the exceeding greatness of his power to us-ward who believe according to the working of his mighty power.
14. **1 Timothy 2:5** For *there is* one God, and one mediator between God and men, the man Christ Jesus . . .
15. **Mark 7:8** For laying aside the commandment of God, ye hold the tradition of men, *as* the washing of pots and cups: and many other such like things ye do.

16. **2 Timothy 2:15** Study to shew thyself approved unto God, a workman that needeth not to be ashamed, rightly dividing the word of truth.
17. **2 Corinthians 4:4** In whom the god of this world hath blinded the minds of them which believe not, lest the light of the glorious gospel of Christ, who is the image of God, should shine unto them.
18. **Isaiah 43:27** Thy first father hath sinned, and thy teachers have transgressed against me.
19. **Ephesians 1:18** The eyes of your understanding being enlightened, that ye may know what is the hope of his calling, and what the riches of the glory of his inheritance in the saints.
20. **Ephesians 1:17** That the God of our Lord Jesus Christ, the Father of glory, may give unto you the spirit of wisdom and revelation in the knowledge of him . . .
21. **Luke 15:7** . . . that likewise joy shall be in heaven over one sinner that repenteth . . .
22. **2 Timothy 2:25** In meekness instructing those that oppose themselves; if God peradventure will give them repentance to the acknowledging of the truth . . .
23. **2 Timothy 2:26** And *that* they may recover themselves out of the snare of the devil, who are taken captive by him at his will.
24. **2 Peter 2:1** . . . there shall be false teachers among you . . .
25. **Ephesians 6:16** Above all, taking the shield of faith, wherewith ye shall be able to quench all the fiery darts of the wicked.
26. **3 John 1:2** Beloved, I wish above all things that thou mayest prosper and be in health, even as thy soul prospereth.
27. **Hebrews 13:5** . . . I will never leave thee, nor forsake thee.
28. **Revelation 13:9** If any man have an ear, let him hear.
29. **3 John 1:4** I have no greater joy than to hear that my children walk in truth.

Chapter 4
The Importance of Knowing and Living the Truth

It has become such common practice for people to contradict the truth that even strong-minded Christians, when teaching or writing about God or the Bible being so wonderful, have actually taken away from his word by changing it. I don't think we even realize the degree of it. God said in six different ways, but always the same message, "the truth will make you free."[1] Most people want to say, "the truth shall set you free." This may seem like a little thing, but God said the same thing six times and he used the word make or made each time. He never once used the word set. Think about the words, made and make, this says once and for all, it is done. You cannot unmake something but you can un-set it, so why put the word set in this verse? God said it bigger than we are saying it. We are watering down his word. Have you ever taken a drink of something after it gets watered down?[2-6]

Here is another verse that is commonly watered down: 1 Peter 4:8, "Charity shall cover the multitude of sins."[7] It is commonly quoted, "Love covers a multitude of sin." The word charity means the love of God in the renewed mind, so why water it down with the word love instead of charity? Take a second to consider the difference. Now think about this: in this day and time, love comes and goes. People say they love you, and then they leave you. They hurt you, lie to you and then they love you so much that they want to change you. We even have biological fathers who are not there for their children. So, because of the love we are accustomed to, it is difficult to understand God our Father's love. This is why we have to renew our minds in order to appreciate and believe his unconditional, never-hurting-us, never-leaving-us and never-forsaking-us kind of love.

As Christians, we all need to be more cautious of what we say or imply. We need to think before we speak, endeavoring to speak truths, because when we don't this is one of the ways Satan can creep in unawares.[8] How important is this? Well, according to God all things come from a spiritual source. It's either from God or it's from Satan. Anything bad or dark or anything that is a lie is from Satan.[9] "God is light and in him is no darkness at all."[10] What gives anyone the right to change God's word, or say things about him that are not true? We hear people say how great God is, but basically what some of those same people are saying is that this wonderful God kills good people,[11] as well as tempts them and tests them. Isn't this double-talk? Just think how confused our children and others around us must be. By not knowing the truth there is room for doubts for God's people. Doubts, worries and fears come from Satan.

Truth and facts should be what children and others are hearing from Christians and their leaders.

Again, I am not against any religion. This is critical; it's God's word that's being tossed around. The only thing that matters is that we are reading and hearing the same rules and promises, and the same truths from our Bibles and teachers, and more important is that we want to know God's truth. Consider for a moment the familiar song that many love and sing, "I once was lost, but now am found, was blind but now I see." How deep are the truths that you want to see? And how important is it to see the whole truth?

My thirteen-year-old daughter knows the word pretty well; at thirteen she is learning to search things and make her own decisions. I am grateful that she is doing this because she has to make it her own truth, not just accept it because I said so. We taught her a long time ago that God wants her to be wise. We have taught her to search all things and understand them before she believes them, and not to follow others just because she wants to be their friend or because it sounds good. Satan was the angel of light and he can, on the surface, make things appear to be light. So search out the truth daily and look for God's truth in every little thing.[12] This way, no one can talk you out of it because you have made it your own.

This is one example: Recently, one of Ashley's teachers died of cancer, and she wanted to go to the funeral. She went with a friend from school and her friend's parents. When she came home we chatted about how it went. She said the preacher said that her teacher was in a better place and that God must have needed another angel, so he brought her home. I explained that this is very common to hear at funerals. Then she began to reason this with me saying, "It made the teacher's husband and her eleven-year-old daughter feel better knowing this, and they were comforted by it." She asked me, what was wrong with believing this if it made them feel better and it helped them get through their loss? I understood her wondering about this, because on the surface it seemed innocent and comforting, so I asked her, "Who does God say is the author of death?"[13, 14]

She said, "Satan is."

"And what does God say happens to a person when they die?" She said, "They are asleep,[15] and when Christ returns to gather us they will raise up."[16-19]

Then I said, "Let's look at this a little closer and see God's bigger truth, and see why it is so important to accept the whole truth. God says the truth makes you free, right? Let's think about how the truth can make us free in this case. This little girl, for one thing, Satan took her mother's life and God is getting blamed for it, right? So, later in her life this little girl could be angry with God. And what if Satan convinced her that she could be in that better place with her mother? This could cause her to want to die herself, or worse yet, what if he could use this to get her to commit suicide at fifteen?"

She agreed that this was all true.

I continued by saying that this could be an open door for Satan to do his business: steal, kill and destroy. Besides those things, if there is a better place to be right now, and if it is with God, why don't we all just go there? I reminded my daughter that if being in heaven right now was available, then why did God say Jesus Christ will come back to gather those who are asleep? If they are asleep in Christ they would already be there and he would not need to gather them in the return. There wouldn't need to be a return if all the Christians who have died are in heaven. She agreed and understood how important the whole truth really is.

This information is documented in 1 Thessalonians 4:13–18. It says,[16-19] "Concerning them which are asleep that believed Jesus died and rose again, the Lord himself shall descend from heaven with a shout, with the voice of the archangel, and with the trump of God; and the dead in Christ shall rise first. Then we which are alive and remain shall be caught up together with them in the clouds, to meet the Lord in the air: and so shall we ever be with the Lord." Verse 18 says for us to "comfort one another with these words."[20]

Now let's look at this with logic. If God is leaving this little girl to grow up without her mother, wouldn't you think she could be angry with God when her mother is not there for her graduation or her wedding day? Not to mention she will not be there to teach her daughter about him (God). Also, she cannot be there to raise her children up in the nurture and admonition of the Lord,[21] the way God advised her to do. God did not say something he didn't mean; this kind of teaching leaves people to think God selfishly took her back so she couldn't do these things after he told her to, and this also leaves people really confused. There is nothing about this believing or teaching that fits with the scriptures. It certainly does not describe the God a little girl is likely to grow up wanting to love, trust and believe in for her health and prosperity, much less any of his other wonderful promises.[22]

Consider all the others who heard those same things. Remember how Satan had almost destroyed me because I had heard things like this? It is still planting seeds for Satan to creep in unaware in the future for a lot of people. God said, "Satan is the author of death."[23] God is taking the blame and Satan is winning all the way around and in more ways than we know. Commonly spoken untruths like this could also have something to do with why so many people do not want to hear about God and his promises. If we do not think about what we are hearing and have not confirmed it for truth, it still remains in our minds and becomes part of what we speak. We are all guilty of telling others what we have heard or read, without studying it for truth. How important is truth? We are intelligent people; we need to establish what we think we know by considering our every thought and lining it up with God's word for truth.

So, how do we know if we are being wrongly taught? The same way we know when a person is telling us a lie. The first clue is when the facts don't fit. Whether it comes from other people, our children or God, the truth is not confusing and it does not have missing pieces.

Let's confirm further these teaching about death according to the word. God's word says in Hebrews 2:14[13] ". . . that through death he [Jesus] might destroy him that had the power of death, that is the devil." The Bible tells us that the last enemy to be destroyed will be death, so from these, we can conclude from God that death is our enemy. In Proverbs 18:21 it says, "Death and life are in the power of the tongue, [the confessions we make are what we receive]."[24] This is God's simple design. There are many things in God's word to confirm that God does not take lives. Think about this: if God is no respecter of persons, then he would not choose one of us at a time to be an angel; choosing her to be with him as one of his angels first would make her more special and him a respecter of persons.[25] Also, God is light and in him there is no darkness at all; doesn't death put a person in darkness? And God said above all things, he wants us to prosper and be in health; doesn't bad health cause death? We are also informed that there is great joy in heaven over one sinner that repenteth.[26] This confirms that God would not take the life of a sinner; if sin brought us death we would all be dead. If you are one who knows the Bible well, you might ask, what about Romans 6:23, "The wages of sin is death . . ."? Well, Matthew 6:24 is only one of several scriptures that says, "no man can serve two masters . . . Ye cannot serve God and mammon." Matthew 6:23 says, "But if thine eye be evil, thy whole body shall be full of darkness," which establishes, that if a person is knowingly walking in sin, he is serving the god of darkness and death and not the God of life and light. At any given moment the God we are serving is the God we have chosen to protect or direct us.

Something else to consider is this: how can we think a loving God and Father could be cruel enough to cause a wonderful woman, and child of his, to suffer a miserable death of cancer, much less the suffering of her family and loved ones? If your father slowly and cruelly killed your mother, would you love, trust and respect him? And how would you feel if someone thought you could do something so evil to your son or daughter? How must God feel knowing that we could think this evil is from him?[27] I do not believe it is intentional, but I do believe we are wrongfully blaming God for Satan's works because of our wrong teachings. For lack of teaching, or wrong teaching, people are finding it easier to blame God, rather than try to explain Satan and feel like a fool trying to explain something we do not understand. And through this whole process we are being destroyed for our lack of knowledge, if these teachings are what we are being taught.[28] We and our children are being kept ignorant of Satan and his devices, and Satan is stealing, killing and destroying God's people. By blaming God, we are also in a way denying that Satan even exists. So we must know and understand God and his word and teach his truth. God's truth does not have contradictions, and the truth will make you free from many of the attacks from Satan that others are vulnerable to because of wrong teaching.[29] We have, like Job, left doors open for Satan.

With God and his word directing our path we can correct these wrongful traditions we have unknowingly allowed.[30] But we must accept the truth and act on it, especially if the Bible and logic both document it.[31]

Scriptures, Chapter 4

1. **John 8:32** And ye shall know the truth, and the truth shall make you free.
2. **Romans 6:18** Being then made free from sin, ye became servants of righteousness.
3. **Romans 6:22** But now being made free from sin, and become servants to God . . .
4. **Romans 8:2** For the law of the Spirit of life in Christ Jesus hath made me free from the law of sin and death.
5. **Galatians 5:1** Stand fast therefore in the liberty wherewith Christ hath made us free, and be not entangled again with the yoke of bondage.
6. **1 Corinthians 7:21** Art thou called *being* a servant? care not for it: but if thou mayest be made free, use *it* rather.
7. **1 Peter 4:8** . . . Charity shall cover the multitude of sins.
8. **Psalms 35:8** Satan catches us off guard and sneaks in unawares.

9. **2 Corinthians 4:6** For God, who commanded the light to shine out of the darkness, hath shined in our hearts, to *give* the light of the knowledge of the glory of God in the face of Jesus Christ.

10. **1 John 1:5** This then is the message which we have heard of him, and declare unto you, that God is light, and in him is no darkness at all.

11. **2 Corinthians 11:14** And no marvel; for Satan himself is transformed into an angel of light.

12. **Acts 17:11** These were more noble than those in Thessalonica, in that they received the word with all readiness of mind, and searched the scriptures daily, whether those things were so.

13. **Hebrews 2:14** . . . that through death he [Jesus] might destroy him that had the power of death, that is, the devil . . .

14. **John 10:10** The thief cometh not, but for to steal, and to kill, and to destroy: I am come that they might have life, and that they might have *it* more abundantly.

15. **1 Thessalonians 4:13** But I would not have you to be ignorant, brethren, concerning them which are asleep, that ye sorrow not, even as others which have no hope.

16. **1 Thessalonians 4:14** For if we believe that Jesus died and rose again, even so them also which sleep in Jesus will God bring with him.

17. **1 Thessalonians 4:15** For this we say unto you by the word of the Lord, that we which are alive *and* remain unto the coming of the Lord shall not prevent them which are asleep.

18. **1 Thessalonians 4:16** For the Lord himself shall descend from heaven with a shout, with the voice of the archangel, and with the trump of God: and the dead in Christ shall rise first . . .

19. **1 Thessalonians 4:17** Then we which are alive *and* remain shall be caught up together with them in the clouds, to meet the Lord in the air . . .

20. **1 Thessalonians 4:18** Wherefore comfort one another with these words.

21. **Ephesians 6:4** And ye fathers, provoke not your children to wrath: but bring them up in the nurture and admonition of the Lord.
22. **3 John 1:2** Beloved, I wish above all things that thou mayest prosper and be in health, even as thy soul prospereth.
23. **1 Corinthians 15:26** The last enemy *that* shall be destroyed *is* death.
24. **Proverbs 18:21** Death and life are in the power of the tongue . . .
25. **Acts 10:34** . . . Of a truth I perceive that God is no respecter of persons . . .
26. **Luke 15:7** I say unto you, that likewise joy shall be in heaven over one sinner that repenteth, more than over ninety and nine just persons, which need no repentance.
27. **Hosea 4:6** My people are destroyed for lack of knowledge: because thou hast rejected knowledge, I will also reject thee . . .
28. **2 Corinthians 2:11** Lest Satan should get an advantage of us: for we are not ignorant of his devices.
29. **Proverbs 3:5** Trust in the Lord with all thine heart; and lean not unto thine own understanding.
30. **Proverbs 3:6** In all thy ways acknowledge him, and he shall direct thy paths.
31. **2 Thessalonians 3:6** Now we command you, brethren, in the name of our Lord Jesus Christ, that ye withdraw yourselves from every brother that walketh disorderly, and not after the tradition which he received of us.

Chapter 5
It's Our Truth, but Only if We Live It

God's word can be simple. Have you ever heard the saying that it's the simple things that confound the wise? We can keep it as simple as light vs. dark, truth vs. lies, positive vs. negative, confidence vs. doubts, if that makes it easier for you to recognize the difference between God and Satan and to know which one is working in your life each day.

God said, "He is light and in him there is no darkness at all."[1] Negatives do not bring light; this means the negative side is always Satan's work. This is one of the easiest and quickest ways to determine truth from God in a given situation. This same truth can confirm any situation.

You may notice as you read this book that I may say something more than once; God did this also. Most of the things he said, he said at least twice. How many times do we tell our children something before they get it? God is no different with us than we are with our children.

There are many that people read the Bible and are familiar with the scriptures. God's word says some are "ever learning, and never able to come unto the knowledge of the truth."[2] We go to church, try to live a good life and to do the right things. People are reading Christian books and listening to sermons on the radio or television. I listen and read them myself because I love the word. Far too often I read or hear what appears to be a great teaching, but in those teachings will be untruths regarding God or his word.

I often wonder how many others are reading or listening, who don't know it's untruth, and it saddens me because those untruths are limiting God in people's lives. God has said for us to "beware of false prophets, which come in sheep's clothing."[3] Some don't even realize that they are wrongly teaching you, if they are convinced of what they have been taught. This is probably the biggest reason for my desire and the purpose of this book: to help others out of the lost state that I was in.

People are becoming familiar with the accounts in the scriptures from hearing them in so many different ways. But we also need to know why God wants us to know the accounts of Job or Ruth or Daniel and so on.[4] What was God's purpose for this information and what is the benefit to you because you know it?

God has a perfect plan and purpose and reason for every word, every verse and every account in the Bible. The reason for all the statements and accounts God gives us is because he knew each and every one of his children would have different situations in their lives and need different answers. In these accounts, we can find ourselves living in similar situations, even now. As I showed earlier in the example of Samson and Delilah and others throughout this book, the same principles and scriptures will always document our life. Which one can you relate to today? God could not leave any of the answers out, so these accounts are in there for our learning. There is not a situation you can find yourself in that God did not give you examples for your personal direction and understanding. In his word, you can find out from God how and why it happened, and what you can do to fix it. Your heart's desire to walk with God and his direction is what will take you to him and his word to find it (those perfect results).[5] This is what God meant when he put my name in Job and said, he did not leave any answers out (doctrine, reproof, correction).[6]

You can be assured that he would not, and did not, give others something he has not made available to you. The only difference between God's children is what we choose to believe and ask him for. God does not think more of any one person than he does another. God will give you what you ask for. He would not have written his word so that we would need a Master's degree in Biblical Study to understand it, or so that our eternal lives would have to be dependent on someone that does.[7] He wrote his word for you.

Do we know why some of his children have more than others do? Why some see signs and some receive miracles, some prosper and some have health if God is no respecter of persons?

The reason for the differences in Christians is not just the knowledge of the Bible itself; it is the understanding and the application. But one of the biggest keys to the answer of these questions is this, "believing ye shall receive."[8] I cannot emphasize this nearly enough. What you believe, good or bad, you will receive. Whether a person is Christian or non-Christian, this law from God will never change. This is why he said in James 1:22, "Be ye doers of the word and not hearers only."

Application simply means to apply and do what you know. When troubles come upon people, no matter the degree, our believing, application and stand on faith determine the outcome.[9]

God's word says, "Satan walks about like a roaring lion, seeking whom he may devour."[10] And this is exactly what he does, he walks about, waiting and watching, looking for an opportunity to devour, also to steal, to kill and to destroy.[11] An example of this in our lives was evidenced as true this past summer.

We have a swimming pool, so most of the time we have many children around. On this particular day, between our children and those of some friends, there were six we were watching. One of my sisters brought over five more under the age of ten. She needed to run to the store, so she came in the house to let me know she would be right back. I knew that Bob was in the pool with them, so I sat at the table writing this book and didn't give it another thought. I didn't even consider that there was now one adult watching eleven children.

What seemed to be only minutes later, one of the teenagers came running in the house screaming, "Carrie, Jimmy has drowned in the pool!" I ran out the door behind her, calling out, "God, please don't let this happen," all the way to the deck. As I came upon them, I saw the most frightful thing I have ever seen or experienced: this frail little child, lifeless and blue-gray in color, on the edge of the pool. Bob was already doing CPR with no response, and by this time, I was on the phone with 911 in a panic. There were kids screaming and crying everywhere and I remember, in the chaos, noticing Ashley and Elizabeth on the outside of the deck, appearing pretty calm.

Bob looked up and said, "Kids go in the house," and he continued compressions and mouth to mouth, with no response. As soon as things were calm, and the kids were out of the way, he said, "God, don't let this child die on me; tell me what to do." It appeared that he was actually lying on him, as he pushed on his little chest and blew in his mouth. Bob told us later that his only thought and instruction at that time was to repeat this three times. Sure enough, the third time, the water released and we heard the most joyous sound I think we have ever heard. The paramedic on the phone asked, "Is that him I hear crying?" As I replied, "Yes," I remember him saying, "That's good, stay calm, the paramedics are almost there."

Hearing the sirens coming closer, I hung up the phone, and Ashley came up and put her arms around me, and said, "Mom, calm down, it will be okay; Elizabeth, Brittany and I have been praying the whole time."

I immediately calmed down, but in the ambulance a few minutes later, watching this tiny four-year-old, I realized there were still numerous things to overcome. I made a call to our prayer line. We call one person and ask him or her to pray and they each call four more people, and so on.

My sister met us at the hospital as soon as she got word. Come to find out she had gone to the store to buy a new swimsuit life jacket for Jimmy, because his was a removable vest and he would not leave it on. In spite of her telling him not to, he had taken it off when this happened.

We knew Jimmy was going to be fine.[12] Although the negatives and concerns were coming from every direction in the emergency room, each one was gone as quick as it came up. He was in ICU through the entire night. By morning he was sitting in a chair watching cartoons and playing with the toys and his teddy bear my sister had brought him. He had eaten a very large breakfast, and watching him, you would never know anything had happened. The doctor even commented on how unusual it was for this quick, perfect outcome, as he released him from ICU to go home that morning.

I tell you these life accounts because there is so little understanding of how and why things like this happen. God has informed us of these answers in his word, but many people are reading right over them. So let's go to God's word and find them, because many people are being left bewildered thinking these things are by chance. Another reason we need to find out how and why this happened is so we can learn from our mistakes. The word warns us, "Be not ignorant of Satan's devices lest he should get an advantage." So if we don't find out why and how something happened, then we remain ignorant and Satan still has the advantage. We'll start with the warning from God that started this story. Satan creeps about like a lion seeking whom he may devour, and another warning, "Satan sneaks in unawares," and yet another, "the thief comes to steal and to kill and to destroy." By these scriptures, we know that it was Satan's doings.

Remember, we are not looking to place blame on anyone, but we need to understand what happened. (Knowledge is power.) Now, how did he catch us off guard and sneak in? Thinking back, I sat at the table not giving it another thought, so I obviously did not pray or thank God for their safety. When I asked the others later, no one else had either, so the god of this world still had an opening. Of all the people out there that day, why Jimmy? According to the word, Satan can only get to us where we have allowed an opening, so he knew where he might be able to get in because of the issues with the life jacket. And he could also see by our actions that we may not have closed that break in the hedge, which allowed him to devour. Satan had to be doing exactly what God says he does. Creeping about and seeking, which means he had to be watching and listening in order to know where the breaks were in the hedge.

No matter how well we know God's word, Satan knows it as well or better. When we are caught off guard, all we have to do is apply what we know, ask God, listen and act, even if we don't understand it at the time. The word says, "Lean not to your own understanding, in all your ways acknowledge him and he shall direct our path."

There are a number of accounts in the word where people have been raised from the dead and even Jesus himself had to remove the unbelievers or doubtful people from the area. One account in particular in the book of 1 Kings 17:19 was about a child who died, and Elijah removed him from the unbelieving mother's presence and he cried unto the Lord God and lay on him three times and the child was raised.[13,14] Is this a coincidence? Could it be the answers from God's word for us explaining why some survive and some don't and the differences in the outcomes?

There is another point to this. Why would Satan be watching us so closely? Because we are Christians, teaching and talking about God and his word all the time. Satan's desire is to cause people to question and doubt what we speak, which is one of his most effective ways to steal the word from people.

This may also explain why many people have heard God's word, gotten excited for a while, and then walked away. Without enough understanding of Satan's devices, he can easily hit people harder with fiery darts, talking them right out of the excitement they had for God's word by causing them to doubt. If they don't know how to turn to the word and understand what God meant in the Bible when he said, "the rain falls upon the just and the unjust."[15] When Satan attacks, people consider and accept what they do know[16] (the old cliché when it rains it pours), and think they are no better with the word than they are without it, and they drift away.

God's word is not the mystery people have made it out to be; we are just not using it to its full benefit and potential. God designed his word with such an awesome perfection that most people are reading right over the simple design and not understanding the personal and individual purpose for everything he said. The Bible is God's direction for each one of his children. He did not design it to be complicated; he designed it to be a personal book of direction for each of his children. As you learn how to find your answers for your life, you will see the magnificence of God's words that are written to you.[16]

Furthermore, as a personal God and your Father, he has made every one of his promises directly to you. You have free will to receive as much or as little as you want from him.

God will not give you what I ask for. He will give you what you ask for. Let me ask you this: if one of your children asks you for something, would you give it to your other child or to the one that asked? There is nothing that our children can ask for that we wouldn't give them if it's good for them. The difference between God and us is that we are limited in what we can give to our children, but God is not limited in the blessings he can give us. His word says, "Ask and it shall be given you; seek and ye shall find; knock and it shall be opened unto you."[17]

Scriptures, Chapter 5

1. **1 John 1:5** This then is the message which we have heard of him, and declare unto you, that God is light, and in him is no darkness at all.

2. **2 Timothy 3:7** Ever learning, and never able to come to the knowledge of the truth.

3. **Matthew 7:15** Beware of false prophets, which come to you in sheep's clothing.

4. **Romans 15:4** For whatsoever things were written aforetime were written for our learning . . .

5. **Psalms 37:4** Delight thyself also in the Lord; and he shall give thee the desires of thine heart.

6. **Mark 11:24** Therefore I say unto you, What things soever ye desire, when ye pray, believe that ye receive *them*, and ye shall have *them*.

7. **Proverbs 12:11** . . . he that followeth vain *persons is* void of understanding.

8. **Mark 11:24** . . . believe that ye receive *them*, and ye shall have *them*.

9. **Ephesians 6:16** Above all, taking the shield of faith, where with ye shall be able to quench all the fiery darts of the wicked.

10. **1 Peter 5:8** Be sober, be vigilant; because your adversary the devil, as a roaring lion, walketh about, seeking whom he may devour . . .

11. **John 10:10** The thief cometh not, but for to steal, and to kill, and to destroy: I am come that they might have life, and that they might have *it* more abundantly.

12. **Proverbs 3:5** Trust in the Lord with all thine heart; and lean not unto your own understanding.

13. **1 Kings 17:19** And he said unto her, Give me thy son. And he took him out of her bosom, and carried him up into a loft . . .

14. **1 Kings 17:22** And the Lord heard the voice of Elijah; and the soul of the child came into him again, and he revived.

15. **Mathew 5:45** That ye may be the children of your Father which is in heaven: for he maketh his sun to rise on the evil and on the good, and sendeth rain on the just and on the unjust.

16. **Matthew 4:4** But he answered and said, It is written, Man shall not live by bread alone, but by every word that proceedeth out of the mouth of God.

17. **Matthew 7:7** Ask and it shall be given you; seek and ye shall find; knock and it shall be opened unto you.

Chapter 6
How to Be a Doer

There are so many teachings and books that tell us how God says we should live, but far too few that teach us how to do that in this day and time, and in the world we are living in today.

If you have gone to church for any length of time and you cannot explain the word of God, or if you do not understand it enough yourself to teach it to others and to your children, then something is wrong.[1] When you have gone to school for years, do you expect to know the subject well enough to use it? Do you expect to get a job and go to work, or do you continue going to the teacher?

Don't misunderstand; not all teachers and churches are wrong. We just need to be cautious that we are being taught God's word, and not traditions. God's word says, in Mark 12:38–39, "Beware of scribes which love to go in long clothing, and love salutations in the market places . . . and the chief seats in the synagogues, and the uppermost rooms at feasts:"[2, 3] In Mark 7:13, he said, "Making the word of God of none effect through your tradition, which ye have delivered: and many like such things do ye."[4] God's word says people honor him with their lips, but their hearts are far from him.[5] It also says in Mark 7:7 " . . . in vain do they worship me, teaching doctrines, the commandments of men."[6] If people are being taught traditions, instead of God's simple direction, this could be why many are still searching.

I attended a Sunday service recently with a friend, at her church. The service was all about how faithful and constant God is. I heard those same things I've been hearing all my life.[7] The preacher mentioned one scripture, and by the time I got there, and read it, he was preaching; come to the Lord, give your life to him, and cast your cares and troubles on him. All through the rest of the service he never referred to the Bible. As I glanced around the church it was so obvious that I was not the only one who was getting very little out of this. I could see the boredom all around us after fifteen minutes, and still on this same subject. I observed from the back pew, wondering how many times they had heard this, and how many left there leaving their troubles on their constant, faithful Father. Also wondering, do they truly expect those troubles to be gone when they get home? Or do many get there and lose a little more hope? If it were as easy as the preachers make it sound, wouldn't life be perfect? I asked my friend how many new people were there. She said, maybe three, and she also said that most of them have been attending this church for years. Toward the end of the service I watched the preacher, to see if he also noticed how many left before the service ended. Maybe he has in the past, I concluded, and this was the explanation for why they did the offerings first. Has this become the traditional church service?

How can we be doers of the word if we remain unlearned? Become a doer. You have a right to ask your teacher questions, and to study those answers. What would happen to the churches if the students also became teachers? Would we still need the teachers? Of course we would. I cannot imagine where my life would be without Chuck (my pastor) or Leonard (my reverend and teacher) and their wonderful patience and teachings. I learn from them and other members of our group continually. There is so much depth in God's word; we will never know it all. If we all hear God's word taught, we should be able to go to any church any time, to meet our brothers and sisters in Christ but more important, to find support, correction, reproof, answers and encouragement so Satan is less likely to catch us off guard.

The word says that "there is safety in the multitude of counselors."[8, 9] We all need to stop making everything a tradition and start doing what the word says: be "apt to teach" the people present, and ready always to give an answer to anyone who asks you a question of the hope that is in you with meekness and fear [respect].[10, 11] If the churches are not doing this, then how can we? Jesus Christ himself taught on the side of a mountain, or wherever there were people. He taught them, and those he taught, taught others. When we are taught with enough understanding, we can also share it with others.

I love God and his word and my desire is to reveal him to others, like Jesus did. He never said, "Come to the church or the temple on Sunday and I'll teach you." Actually, the word says they taught in the temple and in houses daily.[12] Why? Because people have daily needs.[13] In this day and time many people cannot wait until Sunday to get answers if the need hits them on a Tuesday. Usually Satan has ripped their world apart and has gotten them off track by Saturday, so they don't show up to church on Sunday. Do we realize that one of the first things God did when Christ died was rip the veil in the temple?[14] This veil in the temple was placed there to divide the elders of the church who were considered to be the holiest from the common people.[15] So God's message to us when he ripped the veil is that we would be equal in Christ, and it was fulfilled the day he was raised and became available the day of Pentecost. This understanding comes from Jesus instructing the apostles to wait for the promise from the Father to be fulfilled.

If so many of God's children were not so confused, we could be doing the same things that Jesus and the apostles were doing.[16] Jesus said we can do all the things he did, so they are our examples: teaching wherever there is need, healing those who are lame or blind, and casting out devil spirits—and these are just a few things we could be doing. We could be teaching those we meet on Tuesday outside of the church. It may even be someone you work with. I know this may sound a little far-fetched, or like a dream, but what other dream are we chasing? This is what the Bible says; aren't these the same things we are going to church and Bible studies to hear about? We must believe and have faith in God and his word or we wouldn't still desire to hear about them. Imagine the result if believers started walking with the boldness and the power that we have been given.

The word says his servants are to be living examples of these things which are established in the scriptures, so when he gives direction to his servants (read it closely), what do you have? Read the following verse, as if it is addressed to you, with your name instead of "they" and your, for "thine." We are God's servants, and it's his word we are to speak with all boldness. He tells us " . . . and grant unto [God's] servants, that with all boldness [your name] may speak [his] word, by stretching forth [your] hand to heal; and that signs and wonders may be done by the name of [his] holy child Jesus."[17, 18] This is you if you are his servant. The old English is not that difficult if you read for understanding of what he said. Acts 5:42 says, "And daily in the temple and in every house, they ceased not to teach and preach Jesus Christ."[12] People in our day should be talking about Jesus Christ and God's word like they did in the days of the first apostles. We have people in this day who are called to be apostles, teachers and prophets, and we are not given less ability than they were.

The word also says, "Now there are differences of administrations,"[19] which in simple terms can be likened to the administrations of the presidents. We had the Bush administration, the Clinton administration, etc. Administrations are periods of time in which we live. We are living in the same administration that the apostles lived in, after Jesus Christ was resurrected. This is called the Church administration.[20] It started the day of Pentecost and it will not change until Jesus Christ returns to gather those who are faithful in him (which is Christ).[21-24] God did not put all these things in his word to tease us. He was informing us with direction of the things he gave us; in order for us to understand and believe that we can and should be doing the things the first apostles did.[25] This is why it says, "For it is written: the promise is unto you, and to your children and to all that are afar off."[26] That includes you and me.

The word also says, "But when that which is perfect is come, then that which is in part shall be done away."[27] "That which is in part" is everything that was given to the apostles the day of Pentecost.[28] They received the Holy Spirit (Christ in them) and spoke in tongues that day.[29] The day of Pentecost was the first day that it was possible for anyone to be born again of the spirit. God knew we would need the power tools that he calls manifestations. Don't let anyone talk you out of them. These power tools were given to this administration.[30] They give us the knowledge, wisdom and ability to defend ourselves against spiritual matters until Christ returns to gather us. This is when that which is perfect will come. Then, at that time, we who believe in Christ will all be like Christ, that is, spirit beings with a new body. That's when things will be perfect and we will no longer need the manifestations, and we will be in a new administration. Until then, we need to claim and utilize what we have been given, because too many of God's children are lost, not knowing where to go.

In today's world, if we truly follow and understand the instructions in God's word and its purpose instead of stumbling around trying to find better ways to do what he originally instructed, we might be able to find a man of God to talk to on a Thursday, and maybe the doors to our temples wouldn't be locked.

This really happened to me one time when I was in great need of comfort. I felt lost, defeated and alone and I didn't know where else to go. I ended up at the nearest church hoping to find answers, but I found the door locked and no one there. Since I was obviously still alone and my troubles were yet on my shoulders, with no one to talk to, I sat in the parking lot for a while thinking. I left eventually with the realization that I just needed to "get tougher." Years later, I found God through someone who I worked with, outside of a church. I am so grateful for his boldness to say, "Do you know who Jesus Christ is?" and for his understanding it enough to teach me. How sad, considering how many times I did attend different churches, and how open my heart was for God, that it took me thirty-two years. But the saddest part of all was that I couldn't find God, in what I thought was his house.

This is why, since I have learned the word of God, I have shared it with so many. In doing so, I have also found that many people think they are under the laws of the Old Testament, but in Romans 15:4 it says, "For whatsoever things were written afore time were written for our learning that we through patience and comfort of the scriptures might have hope." And in Romans 10:4 it says, "For Christ is the end of the law for righteousness to every one that believeth."[31] So those laws were done away in Christ. God also said, "You are justified, and no longer dead in trespasses and sin."[32-34] The word "justified" means "just as if you never sinned." You should not ever be in trespasses and sin and in self-condemnation, thinking you cannot be good enough for God. This limits you with the promises God made to you. So hold on to what God has said: "You are justified." The instant you confess Christ as your savior and believe in your heart that God raised Christ from the dead, you shall be saved. Read Romans 10:9–10. Christ died to take away your sins and he saves those who believe in him.[35, 36] Don't let anyone keep you from knowing the great love that your Father has for you. At your fingertips, you have a locked box full of many things he gave you. Understanding him and his word is your key to unlock it.[35]

I ask you again, why are so many confused? We are listening to the sermons and teachers, who are there to teach us God's word, and they talk for a half hour and use one scripture. This does not explain the details of what we have and how to use it. The word of God is designed to use as many scriptures as needed to describe a situation in your life, and how to correct it, including those you still have when you get home from church. This is when you are supposed to be able to be a doer of what you learned from the teacher.

Have you ever tried to correct a situation in your life using one simple answer? Like I have shown in my life examples, God's word is designed to use many scriptures and the accounts to find the answers for your individual situation. One part of your answer may be in Daniel and another may be in Matthew and so on. For example, if a person has a problem with drugs, marriage, children and the list goes on, can you come up with one answer for 100 percent repair and correction? If it were that easy, we wouldn't have problems.

Depending on the individual situation, you could have a number of things to overcome. For example, doing drugs is one problem and that problem can cause overwhelming debt. Now they have two, and from that you can start lying (three) and stealing (four), you can lose your home (five), and people won't trust you (six). Some people lose their children (seven). Some have guilt to overcome (eight). Some may be in jail (nine) and then they may not feel worthy (ten). The people they love have to let go and forgive (eleven). These lists go on and on, depending on how deep you are in. If you stop doing the drugs, all of your problems will not go away; you need at least eleven answers. This is the same with marriage or any other issue. Like throwing a pebble in the water, a rippling effect happens. This is why you can have a great marriage, and then something happens, and before you know it, you have a hundred things to repair and overcome. Most times it will take more than one answer to get everything back to 100 percent. Think about this. Likeminded means to think the exact same as someone else. Can you talk to and agree with your spouse if you see things two different ways and you are not likeminded? No, so you have a problem. Just knowing that God's word says you have to be likeminded does not make you likeminded. You still have to find an answer that will get you likeminded. Not even turning to God can be the one answer unless you let him direct every issue you have. So even if you turn to God, you have at least two answers. Because if you acknowledge him you only have one answer for two issues, you still have to let him direct your path. You have to do both for correction.

God's word has our individual answers for doctrine, reproof and correction for even the tiniest piece of our imperfection, for 100 percent perfection. It was not given just so we would go to church on Sundays to hear about how good and perfect life should be. But isn't that exactly where our traditions have brought us? No matter what our situation is, God gave us specific, individual directions to get back on track. Finding your daily answers from God is not as difficult as you may think. If you agree together that what God's word says will settle it, and then find those answers, you become likeminded, and the rest is easy. God tells you what to do, and you do it together. I like the way our two-year-old says it when we tell him this is what we are going to do: "Oh, okay."

Finding God's answers is easier than you may think. Many of the keys to utilizing and living by the Bible may have been mentioned to us through teachings, but do we understand them enough to use them? One example of this is a Bible concordance; many have heard of them. But how many truly know their purpose, or how to use them? They are a great tool, not just for studying God's word, but also finding our answers.

A concordance is basically a dictionary for the Bible. Most every word in the Bible is listed with the suggested meaning of the word and the Greek or Hebrew word it was translated from. The scriptures are listed where each word was used in the Bible. This is helpful in finding scriptures when you need them, but another use for a concordance is to find answers for a given situation. Look up words that describe your situation and read the scriptures listed, then find the ones that sound familiar or might describe your situation. Go to the Bible and read the substance and context. Continue this pattern until you find your answers. Don't forget to thank God for showing them to you in the name Jesus Christ (wisdom from above); this is how to receive the spiritual wisdom. For then he opened their understanding, that they might understand the scriptures.

If you have a ripple in your life, no matter how impossible things may seem, the Bible says, with God, all things are possible. You have to trust and allow him to direct (he is the pilot, not the co-pilot). I am so thankful to those who have taught me God's word, and I would not be where I am today had they not taught me keys that helped me understand the word. But I know I would not have known it so deep in my heart and with such understanding had God not shown it to me.[37] So even though I share these keys with you, the full understanding can only come from the spiritual wisdom and knowledge God made available to you.[37, 38] This is an individual wisdom. He has told us about this numerous times in his word, like when the word says, "... not in words which man's wisdom teacheth,"[39] and also "for the wisdom of this world is foolishness."[40] These are just a few scriptures to document that worldly wisdom is different then spiritual wisdom.

In 1 Corinthians 3:6, Paul said, "I have planted, Apollos watered; but God gave the increase."[41] No matter how diligently a person tries to teach you, they can only plant a seed or spark an interest (like Paul did), or water an existing seed someone already planted, which means to teach you more (like Apollos did). You have to desire the spiritual understanding, and then God will give you the increase. No preacher or teacher can give it; it's your truth, if you choose to live it.

Scriptures, Chapter 6

1. **James 1:22** But be ye doers of the word, and not hearers only, deceiving your own selves.

2. **Mark 12:38** . . . Beware of the scribes, which love to go in long clothing, and *love* salutations in the marketplaces . . .

3. **Mark 12:39** And the chief seats in the synagogues, and the uppermost rooms at feasts . . .

4. **Mark 7:13** Making the word of God of none effect through your tradition, which ye have delivered: and many such like things do ye.

5. **Mark 7:6** . . . This people honoureth me with *their* lips, but their heart is far from me.

6. **Mark 7:7** Howbeit in vain do they worship me, teaching *for* doctrines, the commandments of men.

7. **2 Timothy 3:7** Ever learning, and never able to come to the knowledge of the truth.

8. **Proverbs 11:14** Where no counsel *is*, the people fall: but in the multitude of counsellors *there is* safety.

9. **Proverbs 24:6** . . . and in multitude of counsellors there is safety.

10. **1 Timothy 3:2** A bishop then must be blameless, the husband of one wife, vigilant, sober, of good behaviour, given to hospitality, apt to teach . . .

11. **2 Timothy 2:24** And the servant of the Lord must not strive; but be gentle unto all *men*, apt to teach, patient . . .

12. **Acts 5:42** And daily in the temple, and in every house, they ceased not to teach and preach Jesus Christ.

13. **1 Peter 3:15** But sanctify the Lord God in your hearts: and be ready always to *give* an answer to every man that asketh you a reason of the hope that is in you with meekness and fear . . .

14. **Matthew 27:51** And, behold, the veil of the temple was rent in twain from the top to the bottom.

15. **2 Corinthians 3:14** But their minds were blinded: for until this day remaineth the same *vail* untaken away in the reading of the old testament; which vail is done away in Christ.

16. **Philippians 4:13** I can do all things through Christ which strengtheneth me.

17. **Acts 4:29** . . . and grant unto thy servants, that with all boldness they may speak thy word.

18. **Acts 4:30** By stretching forth thine hand to heal; and that signs and wonders may be done by the name of thy holy child Jesus.

19. **1 Corinthians 12:5** And there are differences of administrations . . .

20. **Mathew 24:34** Verily I say unto you, This generation shall not pass, till all these things be fulfilled.
21. **Acts 2:1** And when the day of Pentecost was fully come, they were all with one accord in one place.
22. **1 Thessalonians 4:14** For if we believe that Jesus died and rose again, even so them also which sleep in Jesus will God bring with him.
23. **Mathew 24:42** Watch therefore: for ye know not what hour your Lord doth come.
24. **Mathew 24:45** Who then is a faithful and wise servant, whom his lord hath made ruler over his household to give them meat in due season?
25. **Mathew 24:46** Blessed *is* that servant, whom his lord, when he cometh shall, find so doing.
26. **Acts 2:39** and the promise is unto you and to your children, and to all that are afar off . . .
27. **1 Corinthians 13:10** But when that which is perfect is come, then that which is in part shall be done away.
28. **Acts 2:3** And there appeared unto them cloven tongues like as of fire, and it sat upon each of them.
29. **Acts 2:4** And they were all filled with the Holy Ghost, and began to speak with other tongues, as the Spirit gave them utterance.
30. **1 Corinthians 12:7** But the manifestation of the Spirit is given to every man to profit withal.
31. **Romans 10:4** For Christ *is* the end of the law for righteousness to every one that believeth.
32. **Isaiah 43:26**.declare thou, that thou mayest be justified.
33. **1 Corinthians 6:11** And such were some of you: but ye are washed, but ye are sanctified, but ye are justified in the name of the Lord Jesus, and by the Spirit of our God.
34. **Ephesians 2:1** And you *hath he quickened*, who were dead in trespasses and sins . . .

35. **Romans 10:9** That if thou shalt confess with thy mouth the Lord Jesus and shalt believe in thine heart that God hath raised him from the dead thou shalt be saved.
36. **Romans 10:10** For with the heart man believeth unto righteouness, and with the heart, confession is made unto salvation.
37. **James 3:17** But the wisdom that is from above is first pure, then peaceable, gentle, *and* easy to be intreated, full of mercy and good fruits, without partiality, and without hypocrisy.
38. **Luke 24:45** Then opened he their understanding, that they might understand the scriptures . . .
39. **1 Corinthians 2:13** . . . not in the words which man's wisdom teacheth, but which the Holy Ghost teacheth . . .
40. **1 Corinthians 3:19** For the wisdom of this world is foolishness with God . . .
41. **1 Corinthians 3:6** I have planted, Apollos watered; but God gave the increase.

Chapter 7
Why Aren't God's Law's Enough for Us to Live By?

Philippians 3:16 says, "let us walk by the same rule, let us mind the same thing."[1]

Imagine how good and simple life would be if everyone we know and deal with each day strived to live by the word and to be a true Christian according to God. Many people can't even live by God's laws, and others keep making more laws rather than simply enforcing the ones we have already been given. Just make new ones that will fix it. Just one simple example of this, which most of us can relate to, would be this: "Be not drunken with strong drink."[2] Notice it does not say, "Do not drink." To the contrary, the word says, "a little wine for thy stomach's sake."[3] By following God's laws, the only drunk drivers who would harm someone would be the ones breaking God's laws. And he says we reap what we sow,[4] and vengeance is mine saith the Lord;[5, 6] he also said that he will bruise Satan under our feet shortly.[7] So he has made his laws of punishment for those who do. Bringing this captive to God's other laws confirms this even further: that God's laws will be enough if we all live by them. If the person drinking loved God first, he would be walking with God.[8] So God would tell him his individual limit and he would listen and obey. God even gave us laws for a backup if someone who is in fellowship with him goes over the safe limit. Because if they loved their neighbor as their self,[9] they wouldn't drive, for consciousness of others' safety. Is it possible that if more people were praying daily for others, God could stop Satan from taking so many of our loved ones, or God could take care of things his way, and we wouldn't be so consumed with anger and hurt, or laws and punishments? Every one of God's promises and laws covers a Christian's walk. We just need to teach more people how to love God first, and walk in his truths and his laws.

To have this available, we as Christians must come together and live by his truth and his every word. One way to know the truth for sure is to study and rightly divide God's word.[10] In order for his people to prosper, be in health and see the signs, miracles and wonders, and to receive all of his other wonderful promises,[11] we have to know and accept God's truth and live according to his every word. Matthew 4:4, ". . . man shall not live by bread alone but by every word that proceedeth out of the mouth of God."[12] Does this mean you can't dance, can't sing, can't drink, and can't smoke? God's word tells us in Romans 14:14 about our Christian liberty. Summed up, it says, "I know and am persuaded by the Lord Jesus that there is nothing unclean of itself: but to him that esteemeth any thing to be unclean, to him it is unclean."[13] And verse 23 says, "And he that doubteth is damned if he eat, because he eateth not of faith, for whatsoever is not of faith is sin."[14] The Bible says to make a joyful noise unto the Lord.[15] It also says, "Nothing that goes into the man defiles the man." It is what comes out that defiles.[16] If what comes out are negative confessions, beliefs and actions, those same negatives are what you receive. You are the only one accountable for your choices and actions; this is your Christian liberty. But you should take into account God's every word, and make your choices accordingly.

The Bible also says to study to do your own business.[17] This same scripture applies in other areas of life as well. We should always live by these same principles. In daily life when things come up, we should base our decisions on God's word. This means to think before we act. One time I had a friend ask me to sign a petition against abortion. I considered this for a moment and said, I would rather not. He said, "So you believe in abortions?" I told him that I don't have the right to make that decision for others, not knowing their situations or the reasons for their decisions, and that the Bible tells me to study to do my own business.[17] He debated with me, and said, "This is a child that has a right to live, and what about all the people who cannot have children?" I said, "That may be true," and I pray for them often. I then reminded him that I have an adopted child, and how grateful we are that she didn't abort him. He is one of the greatest blessings in our life. Still, what gives anyone the right to make a decision for her? Should someone else have the right to make decisions for you? Isn't this still a free country? He agreed. And I told him that unless we are willing to be there personally to support her needs for the child with food, diapers, shoes, etc., how can we decide for her? And who will pay for counseling if she needs it in order to give the child up for adoption for whatever her reasons are? She is the only one accountable for what she does, and God has also said for us to "judge not, lest we be judged."[18]

The best we can do for others is to teach the true word of God. Maybe then we wouldn't have so many people with these types of decisions to have to make. Maybe if more of our teenagers knew that God knows their every move, they would think twice before they act. This pregnant woman might not know God. Our job from God is only to pray for her and teach her. Then if she learns how to turn to God, he could work things out to the best for everyone concerned, including her child. Also, think about this. If we tell her she has to bring the child in to the world and the child is raised in an abusive situation, did we do the right thing? Who is responsible?

Something else to consider is this: You sign this petition, and it passes as a law. Your wife or daughter is raped and becomes pregnant. Now you have to go to court and tell everyone your business in order to make a private decision. He agreed that this was all true and we continued a great conversation about God's word.

It may not always be easy to make a stand, but people should because we are losing so much of our freedom of choice and speech for these types of things. Another example of this is the seat belt law. I thought God was the protector. I believe we would all be safer if the law was for everyone to pray before driving. What gives others the right to say my family is safer with a seat belt than a prayer? I am not against others making their own choices. But I personally know several people who did not survive an accident because of the seat belt, and one of them was an infant. The point I maker here is this: give us *all* the facts and our *freedom* of choice. We should not be for or against new laws, but we should be against laws that tell people what to do when it does not affect others, especially when they go against God's laws. Besides, the next law may go against what you would choose, or it could be that the Ten Commandments and the Bible will not be allowed in our homes. They have already taken them out of our courts. Where and when will the new laws end? God has already covered any new law we can come up with.

Jesus Christ himself said in Matthew 22:37–40, you shall love the Lord your God with all your heart, and with all your soul, and with all your mind. This is the first and great commandment, and the second is like unto it, you shall love your neighbor as yourself. And on these two commandments hang all the law and the prophets.[19-21] This was said again in Luke 10:27, you shall love the Lord your God with all your heart, and with all your soul, and with all your strength, and with all your mind; and your neighbor as yourself.[8] Then . . . he said unto him, you have answered right; this do and you shall live.[22]

How many of us have had an oops while driving or sat at a stop sign too long according to the person behind us with the horn, and on other days been the one with the horn? I wonder how many of us think to pray for the other one to have a better day after we honked, or do we remain as irritated as it sounded? Wouldn't it be comforting to know someone was praying for us when they notice we are having a less-than-perfect day? Things like this are examples of loving your neighbor as yourself.

You are the best in God's eyes, no matter what you have done. He thinks no more of a Biblical scholar than he does of someone who is not. Remember, God looks upon and knows your heart, and he said we reap what we sow. If you have truly turned to him, and you are not receiving all of God's promises, then maybe you do not feel worthy or maybe you are leaving out part of his equation (his every word), which would cause you to limit God in your life. Man has been taught for so long to read fast, and by doing this, we are reading over the small words. In God's word, this is not the way to know him. God is total perfection and so is his direction.

He had a reason for everything he said, how he said it, where he said it, and to whom he said it. We cannot receive the full ability if we are reading over or leaving out the key ingredients. Have you ever left the yeast out of a cake or bread? Trust me, it will not rise to its full potential any more than we will.

Here is something from his word to draw from that tells us how to fix these types of habits we have developed. God tells us to "come unto him as a child."[23, 24] What if you were not given the opportunity to come unto him as a child? To come unto him as a child means meek and eager to learn, without preconceived ideas. Train yourself to read his every word. Think about what you are reading, not just about what you have been taught that it says. Think about all that God's word says he gave us, then ask yourself, is it being taken away, limited, or watered down?

Know that God is your personal Father. He loves you[25] and he is with you at all times, because he said in his word to you that he will never leave you nor forsake you,[26] and you are righteous in his eyes. What holds many of his children back is that most do not know that the second you confess Christ as your Lord and savior, and believe in your heart that God raised him from the dead,[27] you have a clean slate from the sins of your past.[28] This is what is meant by, Christ "redeemed us."[29] He paid the price for our sins;[30] he also said you are justified (just as if you never sinned).[31] Simply thank God for forgiving you[32] and he will cast his remembrance of your sins as far as the east is to the west and he remembers them no more.[33] This is re-established where Jesus Christ on the cross said, Father, forgive them for they know not what they do.

God only holds you accountable for what you know; that's why he looks upon your heart and not just your actions.[34] His word says, thy word have I hidden in mine heart (not your head) that I might not sin against thee (not won't). Know also for a truth that God does not want you to be afraid of him. Many times when the word "fear" is used in the Bible, it would have been better translated from the Greek word "yare" as the word "reverence," which means respect, (this documentation can be located in a Bible concordance). This is also confirmed in the Bible in Isaiah 29:13, ". . . but have removed their heart from me, and their fear toward me is taught by the precept of men."[35]

God wants you to love and respect him; he is your Father, so think of him as being in the same role as you are with your own children. Do you want your children to fear you? If they came to you and said, "I'm so sorry I did that," and you could look upon their heart and knew they truly meant it, how quickly would you forgive them and be there for them even if was to bail them out?

These are just a few of the truths that will make you free. You can have a clean slate with God at any time you choose, just like your children can with you. When you know his true word, you may realize that you're not as bad as you have thought. Having God and his word in your life is a blessing, not a curse or a job. If you want him in your life each day, he will bless your life each day.

Study his word and show yourself approved, a workman who need not be ashamed, rightly dividing the word of truth. God just wants us to know him. He said in Matt 6:33, "But rather seek ye first the kingdom of God and his righteousness; and all these things shall be added to you."[36] He also said, ". . . seek and ye shall find,"[37] and for us to "meditate upon these things; give thyself wholly unto them; that thy profiting may appear to all."[38] Be diligent, and hide his true word in your heart. Don't let anyone talk you into less than he gave, or less than you are.

But remember, Satan does exist. God told us that he steals, kills and destroys, and that he blinds the eyes so that the glorious gospel cannot shine through. Notice God said the word "steal" first. The first thing Satan wants to steal is the truth in God's word, which is your power source to defeat him. Satan will try to convince you that God's promises are not that easy, but God said, "Greater is he that is in you, than he that is in this world." (1 John 4:4) If you are walking in new-found truth, hold on to what God really said and walk in his truth, no matter what Satan or others throw at you. God's word calls them "fiery darts," which he says can be quenched if we put on the whole armor, and take up the shield of faith that he gave us.[39] If we learn to use God's words in our daily walk and conversation, he will direct our path. God said that his word is sharper than any two-edge sword, so we can use it like one. Picture this armor in your mind. When Satan throws a fiery dart, the shield will quench the dart so that it cannot harm you.[40, 41] The word that you know in your heart is your sword. God's word, when you speak it, cuts like a sword to the truth in any conversation or decision. When Satan throws things at you, you don't always have a Bible or time handy; that's why you need to have it in your heart. Because he said it's sharper than any two-edged sword, you cannot lose a battle if you use the word. What is a helmet? It protects your head, which is your mind. So the helmet of salvation is safety when you hold the word in your mind. God's word said to put on the whole armor. It's not placed there automatically because you know him; you have to put it on every day. The breastplate is the knowledge that you are righteous and God has you protected. He cannot protect you if don't have on the whole armor. If you have doubts, worries, or fears, you have taken off your helmet and laid down your shield. If you are not using his every word, your sword is dull. This is why he said to put on the whole armor. Remember God said, "Resist the devil and he will flee from you."[42] He also said, in Romans 16:19 and 20, ". . . I would have you to be wise unto that which is good and simple concerning evil and the God of peace shall bruise Satan under your feet shortly."[43, 44]

If you see yourself as God sees you, and know how much he has given and done for you, it should be easy to see how special he thinks you are. This is God's truth. He loves us so much that he gave his only begotten Son for us. He redeemed us, sanctified us and justified us. He even looks upon our hearts in times of bad judgments. Once we are forgiven, he remembers our sins no more, and he has equipped us with a whole armor.

He wants us to live by his every word not because he is strict, but because his every word is what holds our every answer. And then he called us his beloved, and said he wished above all things that we may prosper and be in health, even as our soul prospers. How much more could our heavenly Father have done to show his love and mercy? He gave us every law we need. We must study to do our own business, trust God and base our decisions on his word.

Scriptures, Chapter 7

1. **Philippians 3:16** . . . let us walk by the same rule, let us mind the same thing.
2. **Ephesians 5:18** And be not drunk with wine, wherein is excess: but be filled with the Spirit . . .
3. **1 Timothy 5:23** Drink no longer water, but use a little wine for thy stomach's sake, and thine often infirmities.
4. **Galatians 6:7** Be not deceived: God is not mocked: for whatsoever a man soweth, that shall he also reap.

5. **Hebrew 10:30** For we know him that hath said, Vengeance *belongeth* unto me, I will recompense, saith the Lord. And again, The Lord shall judge his people.
6. **Romans 12:19** Dearly beloved, avenge not yourselves, but *rather* give place unto wrath . . . I will repay, saith the Lord.
7. **Romans 16:20** And the God of peace shall bruise Satan under your feet shortly . . .
8. **Luke 10:27** Thou shalt love the Lord your God with all your heart, and with all thy soul, and with all thy strength, and with all thy mind; and thy neighbour as thyself.
9. **Matthew 22:39** And the second *is* like unto it, Thou shalt love thy neighbour as thyself.
10. **2 Timothy 2:15** Study to shew thyself approved unto God, a workman that needth not to be ashamed, rightly dividing the word of truth.
11. **Hebrews 2:4** God also bearing *them* witness, both with signs and wonders, and with divers miracles, and *gifts* of the Holy Ghost, according to his own will.
12. **Matthew 4:4** But he answered and said, It is written, Man shall not live by bread alone, but by every word that proceedeth out of the mouth of God.
13. **Romans 14:14** I know, and am persuaded by the Lord Jesus, that *there is* nothing unclean of itself: but to him that esteemeth any thing to be unclean, to him *it is* unclean.
14. **Romans 14:23** And he that doubteth is damned if he eat, because *he eateth* not of faith: for whatsoever *is* not of faith is sin.
15. **Psalms 98:4** Make a joyful noise unto the Lord, all the earth: make a loud noise and rejoice and sing praise.
16. **Mark 7:15** There is nothing from without a man, that entering into him can defile him: but the things which come out of him, those are they that defile the man.

17. **1 Thessalonians 4:11** And that ye study to be quiet, and to do your own business, and to work with your own hands, as we commanded you . . .
18. **Mathew 7:1** Judge not, that ye be not judged.
19. **Matthew 22:37** Jesus said, unto him, thou shalt love the Lord thy God with all thy heart, and with all thy soul, and with all thy mind.
20. **Matthew 22:38** This is the first and great commandment.
21. **Matthew 22:40** On these two commandments hang all the law and the prophets.
22. **Luke 10:28** And he said unto him, thou hast answered right: this do, and thou shalt live.
23. **Mark 10:14** . . . Suffer the little children to come unto me, and forbid them not: for of such is the kingdom of God.
24. **Mark 10:15** Verily I say unto you, Whosoever shall not receive the kingdom of God as a little child, he shall not enter therein.
25. **John 3:16** For God so loved the world, that he gave his only begotten Son, that whosoever believeth in him should not perish, but have everlasting life.
26. **Hebrews 13:5** . . . for he hath said, I will never leave thee, nor forsake thee.
27. **Romans 10:9** That if thou shalt confess with thy mouth the Lord Jesus, and shalt believe in thine heart that God hath raised him from the dead, thou shalt be saved.
28. **Romans 10:10** For with the heart man believeth unto righteousness; and with the mouth confession is made unto salvation.
29. **Isaiah 51:11** Therefore the redeemed of the Lord shall return, and come with singing unto Zion . . .
30. **1 Corinthians 7:23** Ye are bought with a price; be not ye the servants of men.
31. **Isaiah 43:9** . . . let them bring forth their witnesses, that they may be justified; or let them hear, and say, *It is* truth.

32. **Psalms 103:11** For as the heaven is high above the earth, so great is his mercy toward them that fear him.
33. **Psalms 103:12** As far as the east is from the west, *so* far hath he removed our transgressions form us.
34. **Proverbs 21:2** Every way of a man *is* right in his own eyes: but the Lord pondereth the hearts.
35. **Isaiah 29:13** . . . but have removed their heart far from me, and their fear toward me is taught by the precept of men . . .
36. **Matthew 6:33** But seek ye first the kingdom of God, and his righteousness; and all these things shall be added unto you.
37. **Luke 11:9** And I say unto you, Ask, and it shall be given you; seek, and ye shall find; knock, and it shall be opened unto you.
38. **1 Timothy 4:15** Meditate upon these things; give thyself wholly to them; that thy profiting may appear to all.
39. **Hebrews 4:12** For the word of God *is* quick, and powerful, and sharper than any two-edged sword, piercing even to the dividing asunder of soul and spirit, and of the joints and marrow, and is a discerner of the thoughts and intents of the heart.
40. **Ephesians 6:16** . . . wherewith ye shall be able to quench all the fiery darts of the wicked.
41. **Ephesians 6:11** Put on the whole armour of God, that ye may be able to stand against the wiles of the devil.
42. **James 4:7** Submit yourselves therefore to God. Resist the devil, and he will flee from you.
43, **Romans 16:19** . . . but yet I would have you wise unto that which is good, and simple concerning evil.
44. **Romans 16:20** And the God of peace shall bruise Satan under your feet shortly . . .

Chapter 8
Free-Will Choice

According to the word, free will is one of the biggest keys to receiving from God, and many people are not aware of it.[1] God gave us free will, which means that he needs permission to direct our path. God never controls us. God looks upon your heart, so if your heart's desire is to do his will, that desire gives him your permission to direct your path, even when you are out of fellowship with him for a moment. But, if we have chosen to block him out, he cannot override our free-will choice. This is one of God's many explanations as to why miracles happen for some and not for others in times of need. I know this is what allowed God to send an angel to me in the parking lot of the hospital one night.[2]

My husband had been taken in an ambulance when he passed out cold, landing face first on the floor. By the time the paramedics arrived, his blood pressure was 50 over 32. I was in what is referred to in the word as a natural man's state of mind. I know this because I was not even thinking or trusting in God, I was overwhelmed with doubts and fears, and I had not prayed for my husband from my heart. God warns us about being double-minded, and that it will make a man unstable in all his ways.[3] Many negative things had happened throughout the previous few months, and because of the negatives, I was in a negative frame of mind that day. I was double-minded about the outcome of the situation and I had pretty much accepted that my husband might not make it.

I had called one of my sisters for support, and she said she would be right there. They were taking Bob for some x-rays, so I walked outside of the hospital, and an angel walked up behind me and asked me, "Are you okay?"[4]

I did not know who this was at that moment, but as I turned around to reply, every negative response I had was gone and I could not even speak. I could feel my mouth still open with no words, as she immediately began to speak, and said, "You know that God has sent me with a message,[5] don't you?"

All I could say was, "Yes . . ."

With her finger toward me she began her message, saying, "You know the word of God. Use it. This man is going to die if you don't pray and believe for him."[6] She continued speaking in this straightforward manner, reminding me with scripture how Satan had crept in over the last six months of our lives.

She was documenting everything with scripture that I was all too familiar with, reminding me where Satan had gotten in and what we had done to allow it and what we had not done to stop him. On every point she made, she referenced scriptures that we knew, using God's word to make that point. In between each of them she would say, "And you know what I'm talking about." I sure did.

Through the whole conversation to this point, all I could say in response to her was, "Yes . . ." Using God's word, she scolded me harshly, saying things like, "You know that Satan is the author of death and this man is going to die if you do not start praying for him. Use the word of God to stop this.[7] Put on your spiritual armor, walk with your guard up and do not give up. This is a man of God and he has given up. Now you have given up on him too.[8] Start praying for him so God can save him."[8, 9]

She then began to instruct me on several things that we needed to do. As my sister, Jackie, came across the parking lot, she was saying, "There is a father that you need to call."

I finally spoke something other than "Yes." I said, "He does not know his father, should I call his mother?"

She said, in a stern voice, "You don't call Margaret until after."

As I came out of wondering how she knew my mother-in-law's name, she was saying, "Maybe he's a father figure." She turned her attention for the first time to my sister, who had been standing there speechless with her mouth opened in awe of our conversation. She looked at my sister, and then back at me and said, "Your sister, right?"

Not waiting for an answer, she pointed, "And you!" She began scolding her in the same manner as she had me, and in everything she said, my sister's reply was, "Yes . . ."

And she would say, "You know what I'm talking about, don't you?"

"Yes . . ." was the only response.

The last thing the angel said to my sister, as she nodded in my direction, was, "This woman knows the word of God. You listen to her and let her teach it to you so that you can teach the children." She then nodded toward the car that was pulling up beside us and said, "I must go," and stepped into the car. Jackie and I both stood in awe as we watched the car drive off into the distance. Still not saying a word to each other, we both turned and walked into the hospital.

As soon as we got back into the room and sat down in the chairs, Jackie finally broke the silence and blurted out, "Carrie, it's Chuck. The man you need to call is Chuck." Without debate, I headed for the nearest phone, hesitating just long enough to say a prayer. I called Chuck, who is the pastor of our church. From that moment, signs, miracles and wonders were continual for the next eight days; even x-rays came back not showing things that had shown up on the previous x-rays.

I learned a big lesson from this experience. That angel reminded me how important it is to stand on God's every word and not let down our guard. But even when God sends an angel or messenger, we still have free will to choose whether or not we accept the reproof and correction.

From the very first conversation that we had about the angel and what she had said to us, my sister said that the angel told her to teach the children. What part did she leave out? The most important part: learn it so you can teach the children. You cannot teach something you do not understand. You know the funny thing is that this sister knows more than I do in some areas of the Bible. She often wins our Bible trivia game with the names and history, and she has a great love for God, so the angel was referring to her strength and her application.

Again, the whole truth is not always what we want to hear because it's easier to hold on to what we think we already know. Sometimes, if we accept the whole truth that means that we have to change. God is always willing, but our free will choice requires that we want the change.

Remember when I said that God did not leave any answers out?

I will not press her to let me teach her because God gave me a guiding example in the Bible. Jesus Christ himself was not able to teach in his hometown because they knew him as a child, and when he became a man, they knew his background.[8, 10] We can use what we know from God's word to look for his guidance in any situation. This is why God gave us similarities in the accounts in the Bible.

God does not want or expect all of his children to be exactly the same, any more than we would want our children to be the same. God directs our paths, but he still allows us free will to have the right to be individuals, and to make our own choices, without condemnation of ourselves or each other. This is why he gave us so many things to draw from in his wonderful word. This is also why he said he looks upon our hearts.

God does not ever want us to feel less than the best. He gave us accounts in his word to draw our confidence of his approval even when we miss the mark. The following are from God's word, for confidence in knowing that no matter what we do, even if it takes years, God will be there to encourage and support us. To God, it is not when we do it, but that we do, and when we are ready, he welcomes us with great joy.[11] When God called Moses, it took him about forty years to accept the calling, and God waited until he was ready.

In Luke 15, Jesus explains to the Pharisees why he spent so much time with the sinners and he spoke to them in a parable. Of one hundred sheep, if one was lost, wouldn't you leave the ninety-nine and go after the lost one, and rejoice when it was found?[12, 13] Then he told them, likewise, joy shall be in heaven over one sinner that repenteth, more than over the ninety-nine just persons, which need no repentance. My point is, when we fully understand God and his expectations, instead of the world's expectations, or our own,[14] it is easier to believe in his love for us. He has surely shown his love for us, even when we have missed the mark. God has joy when his angels can save us. If we were perfect, we wouldn't need him or them. Why else did God put these accounts in his word if they are not for us to know his direction for us in our daily situations? [15-17]

Scriptures, Chapter 8

1. **Ezra 7:13** I make a decree, that all they of the people of Israel, and of his priests and Levites, in my realm, which are minded of their own free will to go up to Jerusalem, go with thee.
2. **Deuteronomy 31:8** And the Lord, he it is that doth go before thee; he will be with thee, he will not fail thee, neither forsake thee: fear not, neither be dismayed.
3. **James 1:8** A double-minded man is unstable in all his ways.
4. **Matthew 4:11** Then the devil leaveth him, and, behold angels came and ministered unto him.
5. **Revelations 22:6** . . . the Lord God of the holy prophets sent his angel to shew unto his servants the things which must shortly be done.
6. **Mark 16:17** And these signs shall follow them that believe; In my name shall they cast out devils; they shall speak with new tongues . . .
7. **Mark 16:20** And they went forth, and preached every where, the Lord working with *them*, and confirming the word with signs following. Amen.
8. **Mathew 13:58** And He did not many mighty works there, because of their unbelief.
9. **1 Timothy 4:15** Meditate upon these things; give thyself wholly to them; that thy profiting may appear to all.
10. **Mathew 13:57** And they were offended in him. But Jesus said unto them, A prophet is not without honour, save in his own country, and in his own house.
11. **Luke 15:7** I say unto you, that likewise joy shall be in heaven over one sinner that repenteth, more than over ninety and nine just persons, which need no repentance.
12. **Luke 15:3** And he spake this parable unto them, saying . . .
13. **Luke 15:4** What man of you, having an hundred sheep, if he lose one of them, doth not leave the ninety and nine in the wilderness, and go after that which is lost, until he find it?

14. **Colossians 3:23** And whatsoever ye do, do *it* heartily, as to the Lord, and not unto men.
15. **Proverbs 16:1** The preparations of the heart in man, and the answer of the tongue, *is* from the Lord.
16. **Proverbs 16:9** A man's heart deviseth his way: but the Lord directeth his steps.
17. **1 Corinthians 2:14** But the natural man receiveth not the things of the Spirit of God: for they are foolishness unto him: neither can he know them, because they are spiritually discerned.

Chapter 9
Abilities We Have Through Christ

God's word says, "There is therefore now no condemnation to them which are in Christ Jesus, who walk not after the flesh, but after the spirit."[1] In everything we do as Christians, truly walking by the spirit, as long as the spirit is what guides us, we have no condemnation. If we are walking after the spirit, that spirit in us considers and ponders our hearts and thoughts and lines them up with God's word and direction for us.[2] Walking in the spirit means this, through the spirit God reveals direction and we do it. By bringing our every thought captive, we are no longer directing our own path using only our minds.

This is how we have no condemnation. This is part of the reason for the warning from the word when it says, every man is right in his own mind.[3] We are told to trust in him, and lean not unto our own understanding, in all our ways acknowledge him and he will direct our path. One of the areas of direction that we have, about how to keep our mind from clouding the spiritual direction is in Ephesians 4:22, "That ye put off concerning the former conversation the old man;"[4] Ephesians 4:23, "And be renewed in the spirit of your mind;"[5] Ephesians 4:24, "And that ye put on the new man."[6] This means we have to continually renew our mind, and bring it back to God and his word.

Knowing his truth through the spirit gives us confidence to ask him for anything at any time. When we know who we are in Christ and know what he did for us, it gives us confidence and leaves no room for doubt or self-condemnation. We also have more confidence when we know how he is directing us. You can walk in this new light when you bring your every thought to God for his explanation and direction for you. One of the devil's ploys is to keep us feeling unworthy of God's love and forgiveness and his eagerness to take care of us which causes us not to be as quick to turn to God. So as most of us will do when we get desperate for help we turn to God pleading for forgiveness for our sins so we can feel worthy enough to ask him to fix our mess. But the truth is that if our guilt and feelings of unworthiness had not kept us from asking, or simply giving him permission, he would have fixed it without all the pleading.

God said, "Ask and it shall be given you."[7, 8] He did not say, "only if you are worthy." Or if you are sin-free. He also said, "And all things whatsoever you shall ask in prayer believing you shall receive." He did not say, "all things except." We limit God by not putting emphasis on the word "all." Don't add or read into what God said, just know what he did say; put a period behind it and take it to the bank.

To have God and his word in our lives is not just to know it; God wants us to understand it so we can use it, and live by it.[9]

God has told us what his Son made available to us. The world tells us of all the wonderful things God will do for you if you know him, if you go to church, if you live a Christian life, if you pray, and if you confess your sins. God simply said that if you ask, it shall be given. The truth is, God, through Jesus Christ, already did (past tense) give to us all things,[10] and God's written word tells us what those things are. All we have to do as his children is believe and live by what is written.[9]

One of the greatest things God gave his children through Christ was a gift. 1 Peter 4:10 says, "As every man hath received the gift;" within that gift is a box of tools. God's word tells us not to neglect the gift that is in us,[11] and Satan has cleverly kept this from many of God's people for thousands of years. As with many other things in God's word, Satan has twisted it, limited it, disguised it and watered it down in every way he could. This is the same power Christ had that is now in us (Christ in you). Satan does not want you to use this power that you have. Do you remember what Jesus Christ said, "The works that I do shall ye do also"?[12] He caused the blind to see, made the lame walk, he walked on water, miracles took place that fed thousands. He prophesied, received revelation, cast out devils and went about doing his Father's business and teaching the living word, just

Abilities We Have Through Christ

to name a few. And then he said, "Greater than these can you do also because I go unto my Father."[12] Trust me, Satan does not want us to know how to do the things Christ did, much less the greater things he mentioned. Like he did with Eve,[13-15] Satan has talked people right out of the manifestations (our box of tools) that came with the gift God gave us (past tense).[16] Remember, Jesus Christ also said, "That you shall be endued with power from on high."[17]

Throughout the years, Satan has even managed to keep this from most of the teachers, because they only know what they have been taught from their teachers. All of the things that God said we can do seem so out of our reach and are kept at a distance. I am going to explain in simple terms what has been given to every born-again person who has Christ in them. Now, understand that the world and different religions have watered down the manifestations (this box of tools)[18] and talked many people out of believing they are for us. Many of the people that *have* been taught that these things are available have been taught that God only gives them *one* of these tools, or manifestations. So, many of the people who *do* know they are available to us are limiting the usage of them because of wrong teaching or lack of understanding.

God gave each of us one gift; it is the Holy Spirit, "Christ in you." Within this gift are nine manifestations (power tools) that we can use in this world to defend ourselves against Satan.[19] We can stand strong in this world and walk with power. It is this same power that Christ had. The greater things he mentioned that he could not do are listed in those same nine manifestations. These manifestations are listed in 1 Corinthians chapter 12 and they are: word of wisdom, word of knowledge, faith, gifts of healing, working of miracles, prophecy, discerning of spirits, diverse kinds of tongues, interpretation of tongues.[20] Because God said that he is no respecter of persons,[21, 22] it does not make sense that God would give one of the manifestations to me and another to you. What if one of his children has been injured? I am there, and you are not. If God gave you the manifestation of healing and me the manifestation of wisdom, I would be wise enough to know what to do, but *I* would not have the ability, because he gave *you* the gift of healing. God gave all nine to each of us to use, so we can use any or all according to time and need. So don't allow yourself to be limited or let other people talk you out of all that God has given to you. In order to document what I have just given the sum and substance of, we need to start this subject study in 1 Corinthians 12:1 which says, "Now concerning spiritual *gifts* brethren, I would not have you ignorant." Note: the word "gifts" is in italics. This means the translators added it. The bottom line is, God said that he does not want us to be ignorant, which means unknowledgeable, about these spiritual matters, or gifts. God then explains them and names them and gives us direction on how to use them, through the next three chapters in the Bible.

1 Corinthians 12:7 says, "But the manifestation of the spirit is given to every man to profit withal." The word "manifestation" means to bring something into evidence, which is something you can see, hear, taste, smell, or touch. So the manifestation is given to every man for profit. Verses 8–10 name these manifestations, or evidences, that you can see, hear, taste, smell, or touch. You can profit from any one of these if you choose. Verses 8–10, "For to one is given by the Spirit the word of wisdom: to another the word of knowledge by the same Spirit. To another faith by the same Spirit: to another, gifts of healing by the same Spirit to another the working of miracles to another prophecy; to another discerning of Spirits to another divers kinds of tongues, to another interpretation of tongues."

Many teach that God divides these out to his children because of the way it is written, "For to one is given, and to another is given," and so on. But that contradicts a number of other things God's word has said. "I can do all things through Christ which strengtheneth me," and God being "no respecter of persons," are only two of many. How could he justify giving you faith and giving someone else working of miracles and so on? Remember, he has also said that "it's not of works lest any man should boast." These only name a few of the contradictions, but with that in mind, let's continue to read the next verse. Verse 11 says, "But all these worketh that one and selfsame Spirit, dividing to every man severally as he will."[23] Who is the "he"? Does God will them, or does man? Man is the nearest noun, and God gave them, (past tense). He does not will them. So this says as he (the man) wills. We can use any one of the nine when we need them. Our individual belief and application is the only thing that limits them, (free-will choice) so don't let anyone tell you that you can't.

Most of us have heard of the day of Pentecost, but do we truly understand what happened that day, according to the word of God?

Of the nine manifestations there are only two mentioned that pertain to the power given to us (God's children) that Jesus Christ himself could not do. These are the "greater things" that we can do. The reason he could not do them was because they were not available until the day of Pentecost, which was after his resurrection. (The day of Pentecost was a celebration feast that took place fifty days after the Passover.) In Acts 1:4, Jesus had instructed the apostles to go and tarry at Jerusalem until the promise of the Father, and he told them that they would be endued with power from on high.[17-24] Acts 2:1 says, "And when the day of Pentecost was fully come."[25] Verse 4 tells us they all spoke in tongues after they received the Spirit.[26] Speaking in tongues and the interpretation of tongues is the [greater things] Jesus Christ could not do, because they were not available until that day. God gave us three chapters in his word to direct us in the usage of the manifestations of the gift. Man is the one that translated it *"gifts,"* which is why it is in italics in the King James Bible. Our individual abilities from that one gift are listed with complete instructions for us in 1 Corinthians chapters 12, 13, and 14. God gave us numerous accounts on this subject that spell out in black and white what Christ made available to us and how to use it.

Some denominations have taught that these things were given to the apostles only and not to us because of what the word says in 1 Corinthians 13:10, "But when that which is perfect is come then that which is in part shall be done away."[27] But that which is perfect has not come yet, because Jesus Christ has not gathered us in the return.

Satan has been setting the pace for so long, and most people do not want to acknowledge his existence. We can no longer believe that God exists and yet not believe what God has told us about Satan. The only way to defeat Satan in your life is to learn his devices. The quickest way to do this is for us to train ourselves to see all things in black and white, and realize that if it is not truth, it is a lie. Satan is talking us out of the truth everyday, and people are blind to it.

God has done his part; he gave us his word and said he does not lie. If we learn to resist Satan, he has to flee from us.[28] Everything that we do has rules: governments, schools, driving, sports, etc. God's word is our rulebook to the whats, whys and hows in life. We should train ourselves to bring everything to God's word and draw our answers from him. Stand on it like Christ did, no matter what others say or think.

Jesus Christ himself is the one who told us we can do all the things he could do, and even greater things than he did, because he went unto his Father.

Together, we could change things in this world by using the power that is in us, and the manifestations, to start doing the things that Christ did because he said, "You are of God little children and have overcome them, because greater is he that is in us than he that is in the world."[29] His examples for us are written in his word, and he tells us in Luke 1:37, "For with God nothing shall be impossible."[30]

We cannot change the inevitability of what is written. It is written that there is a wrath to come, but if enough of us start teaching and living as examples, we can change the quality of life and living of the believers until Jesus comes to gather us in the return. Also know that the Bible documents that we will be spared from the wrath to come. This means that Jesus Christ will gather us before the worst happens. You can take comfort in knowing this. 1 Thessalonians 1:10 says, ". . . Jesus, which delivered us from the wrath to come."[31] Acts 2:27 says, "The Holy ones shall not see corruption"[32] and in Malachi 3:17 it says, "And they shall be mine, saith the Lord of hosts, in the day when I make up my jewels; and I will spare them, as a man spareth his own Son that serveth him."[33]

Scriptures, Chapter 9

1. **Romans 8:1** *There is* therefore now no condemnation to them which are in Christ Jesus, who walk not after the flesh, but after the Spirit.

2. **Colossians 1:27** To whom God would make known what *is* the riches of the glory of this mystery among the Gentiles; which is Christ in you, the hope of glory . . .

3. **Proverbs 21:2** Every way of man is right in his own eyes: but the Lord pondereth the hearts.

4. **Ephesians 4:22** That ye put off concerning the former conversation the old man . . .
5. **Ephesians 4:23** And be renewed in the spirit of your mind . . .
6. **Ephesians 4:24** And that ye put on the new man . . .
7. **Mathew 7:7** Ask and it shall be given you; seek and ye shall find; knock and it shall be opened unto you.
8. **Mark 11:24** What things soever ye desire, when ye pray, believe that ye receive them, and ye shall have them.
9. **Matthew 4:4** . . . It is written: Man shall not live by bread alone but by every word that proceedeth out of the mouth of God.
10. **Philippians 4:13** I can do all things through Christ which strengtheneth me.
11. **1 Timothy 4:14** Neglect not the gift that is in thee.
12. **John 14:12** "Verily, verily I say unto you, He that believeth on me, the works that I do shall he do also; and greater works than these shall he do; because I go unto my father."
13. **Genesis 2:16** And the Lord God commanded the man, saying, Of every tree of the garden thou mayest freely eat.
14. **Genesis 2:17** But of the tree of the knowledge of good and evil, thou shalt not eat of it: for in the day that thou eatest there of thou shalt surely die.
15. **Genesis 3:1** . . .Yea, hath God said, Ye shall not eat of every tree of the garden?
16. **Ephesians 2:9** Not of works, lest any man should boast.
17. **Luke 24:49** And, behold, I send the promise of my Father upon you; but tarry ye in the city of Jerusalem, until ye be endued with power from on high.
18. **1 Corinthians 12:1** Now concerning spiritual *gifts* brethren, I would not have you ignorant.
19. **1 Corinthians 12:7** But the manifestation of the Spirit is given to every man to profit withal.

20. **1 Corinthians 12:8–10** For to one is given by the Spirit the word of wisdom; to another the word of knowledge by the same Spirit; To another faith by the same Spirit; to another the gifts of healing by the same Spirit; To another working of miracles to another prophecy; to another discerning of spirits to another *divers* kinds of tongues; to another the interpretation of tongues.

21. **Romans 2:11** For there is no respect of persons with God.

22. **Acts 10:34** I perceive that God is no respecter of persons . . .

23. **1 Corinthians 12:11** But all these worketh that one and self same Spirit, dividing to every man severally as he will.

24. **Acts 1:4** . . . that they should not depart from Jerusalem, but wait for the promise of the Father . . .

25. **Acts 2:1** And when the day of Pentecost was fully come, they were all with one accord in one place.

26. **Acts 2:4** And they were all filled with the Holy Ghost, and began to speak with other tongues, as the Spirit gave them utterance.

27. **1 Corinthians 13:10** But when that which is perfect is come, then that which is in part shall be done away.

28. **James 4:7** . . . Resist the devil, and he will flee from you.

29. **1 John 4:4** . . . Greater is he that is in you . . .

30. **Luke 1:37** For with God nothing shall be impossible.

31. **1 Thessalonians 1:10** And to wait for his Son from heaven, whom he raised from the dead, *even* Jesus, which delivered us from the wrath to come.

32. **Acts 2:27** . . .Thou shalt not suffer thine Holy One to see corruption.

33. **Malachi 3:17** And they shall be mine, saith the Lord of hosts, in that day when I make up my jewels, and I will spare them, as a man spareth his own son that serveth him.

Chapter 10
Understanding the Bible

God's word says in 1 Corinthians 12:27, "Now ye are the body of Christ and members in particular."[1] Verse 28 says, "And God hath set some in the church, first apostles, secondarily prophets, thirdly teachers, after that, miracles, then gifts of healings, helps, governments, diversities of tongues."[2] Verse 29 says, "Are all apostles? Are all prophets? Are all teachers? Are all workers of miracles?"[3] No. One person cannot be the best at everything; which is good because this means we need each other. Each of God's children can have a strong suit (one may be better at teaching, and another may be better at diversities of tongues, etc.), but we are not limited to one. We can develop a strong suit in any or all according to our hearts' desire. Any group of believers would not be as strong without any one of its members. Together, we are a stronger body of Christ, and most people do not know that we each have a part in the body, inside and outside the church. We must understand God and the Bible in order to reach our full potential.

There is key information in the history of the Bible that made a difference for me, and was very helpful in bringing me closer to God. On many occasions I have had conversations with people, and so many are like I was: confused trying to read the Bible. There are some basic things I was taught that helped me to understand the Bible and overcome my confusion and fear of it. Many people I have spoken to are lacking these same basics, so I have included some of the history and details of the word for you, because it could be helpful for your understanding of the Bible.

The Bible is written in two parts: the Old Testament and the New Testament. When Jesus Christ died and God raised him from the dead, all things became new to us that were not available until he was raised. Hebrews 9:15 says, "And for this cause he is the mediator of the New Testament . . ."[4] Also 1 Timothy 2:5 says, "For there is one God and one mediator between God and men, the man Christ Jesus."[5] We can learn from the Old Testament, but the laws in them do not directly apply to us. Jesus Christ fulfilled those laws for us; the Old Testament laws were done away in Christ. Because we are told in Romans 15:4, "For whatsoever things were written aforetime were written for our learning."[6] We can find examples to learn from but our goal is to live in the New Testament laws. Any laws from the Old Testament that apply to us (the church), Jesus Christ brought them back with him, and they are re-established in the New Testament. The Ten Commandments are not listed. But they are restated throughout the New Testament.

Another way to document that this is true, from God, and his word, is to look at the first chapter and first verses in the books of the Bible. Read them carefully for understanding, especially in the New Testament books. Take note when they are addressed to those who are faithful in Christ Jesus. That is you, if you are faithful and know Christ. Corinthians and Ephesians especially are spelled out quite plainly. 1 Corinthians 1:2 says, "To all them that are sanctified in Christ Jesus, called to be saints."[7] The word also says in Hebrew 7:22, "By so much was Jesus made a surety of a better testament."[8] The old was done away in Christ and a better testament was given to us.

To understand the division of Old and New Testament, we have to fully understand what happened in the beginning with Adam and Eve,[9] and what happened in the Garden of Eden. God told them not to eat of the fruit of the tree of knowledge of good and evil or they would surely die.[10, 11] The account tells us that Adam and Eve walked out of the Garden and lived many years because they replenished the earth, starting with Cain and Abel, and they tilled the ground. Now did God lie when he told them they would, "surely die?"[10] No, he did not. Remember in the beginning, when he created man? There were three parts: he formed the body, and then he breathed into him the breath of life, and then he created man in his own image.[12] God's image is spirit,[13] and this is what gives us a three-part being of body, soul and spirit.[9]

Adam and Eve walked out of the garden with a breathing body.[14,]

[15] The breath is the soul, which they still had. They had a body, or they couldn't have walked, so it was the spirit that died. When Jesus Christ died and arose, he gave us back that which Adam and Eve lost (the spirit). The Old Testament was during the time that men did not have that perfect spiritual connection with God, because it was the time period between Adam and Eve and Christ's resurrection. "For God so loved the world that he gave his only begotten Son."[16] Now we can see why Jesus Christ was the price God paid to buy us back from Satan (the god of this world). This price God paid is established in 1 Corinthians 6:20, "For we are bought with a price."[17] It also says again in 1 Corinthians 7:23, "Ye are bought with a price; be not ye the servants of men."[18]

As a father or mother, imagine giving your only son to die for someone. Wow! As a mother myself, I can't even imagine that thought. The following are scriptures to document further that because of the crucifixion of Jesus Christ and him raised, we can have back what Adam and Eve lost, and that is why we are living in the time and books in the Bible referred to as the New Testament.

Hebrews 9:14, "How much more shall the blood of Christ, who through the eternal Spirit offered himself without spot to God, purge your conscience from dead works to serve the living God?"[19]

Hebrews 8:6, "But now hath he obtained a more excellent ministry, by how much also he is the mediator of a better covenant which was established upon better promises."[20]

The books in the Bible called Matthew, Mark, Luke and John are referred to as the Gospels. Matthew and John were two of the disciples who witnessed Jesus Christ's ministry all the way through his death and resurrection. The disciples Mark and Luke were not there from the beginning, but they both witnessed many of the same things and they gave an account of what they each witnessed. But the Bible informs us they were all holy men of God, moved by the Spirit as the Spirit gave them utterance.[21] One area where this is documented in is 2 Timothy 3:16, "All scripture is given by inspiration of God . . ."[22] so what was written was inspired by God, but they used their own vocabulary. When reading the gospels, consider the difference between the vocabulary of a fisherman and a lawyer. Also, the things written happened over a period of time, so these men would not have been standing shoulder to shoulder all this time. So it is important to line up each account with the others so you can put together all the details for the whole story; this is called scripture buildup.

Many things have been passed down to us through teachings and we have accepted them through faith, and things have become embedded in our minds with pictures, sermons and traditions for years. For example, many people, including pastors, know things like the fact that Jesus Christ was not born on the 25th of December. Many people know this but do not teach it because it would not be easy to change the traditions in order to rightly teach the truth. Also do people really want, and are we really ready for the truth? Or have our traditions become more important?

The Bible in its original form was written with no chapters or verses and there was no punctuation of any kind. Punctuation is great for reference, but it has no authority when it comes to rightly dividing the word to find the truth.

The reason this is important to know is that man (translators) added them. This does not mean they are all incorrect, but keep this in mind as you study. It could be the key to eliminate what appears to be a contradiction in the word. This is just one example where punctuation is a factor in what God's word really said. In Luke 23:43, when Jesus was on the cross, he said, "Verily I say unto you, to day thou shall be with me in paradise."[23]

The translators chose to put the comma after "you," which would make this read that he would be with Jesus that very day. For this man to be with Jesus that very day contradicts a number of other things God has told us in his word. The following is one of them: Jesus Christ himself didn't even go there that day, because he was dead for three days and three nights, right?[24]

Now what if this same verse read, "Verily, I say unto you to day, thou shall be with me in paradise"? Now it reads that Jesus said it that day, saying that he would be with him in paradise. By moving a comma over one word, it now makes God's word perfect. Because Jesus told this man he would be with him in paradise, he also confirms again the return. And this would clear up many other contradictions that would occur from this. So, is it possible that the comma was put in the wrong spot? At this point I would like to mention that

Understanding the Bible

this is a big issue in the Catholic-Protestant argument regarding the Catholic concept of purgatory. But purgatory is not mentioned in the Bible and 1 Thessalonians chapter 13 says, we are asleep until the return, to be raised up. My question to them would be, is purgatory somewhere below us? This is why it is so important to understand what you are reading and what you are being taught.

Many parables are used in the word to give us direction, which means they are not literal. These can be hard to understand if we do not know that they are given for us this way so that we can use them for parallel analogy. This is one of Jesus's parables that he used to help God's children in their daily walk: Jesus said, "Cast not your pearls before swine."[25] A swine is a pig, but he is not calling people pigs. This is not literal, it is a parable. So let's do a couple analogies of our daily walk using this parable.

Say you know someone who continually has trouble and they are always in need of help. You have tried to help over and over because it is the Christian thing to do, and, as a Christian, you want to help and to do the right thing. With this parable, Jesus is telling us to consider if what they think they need will really help them. If you give or loan money to a person, and you know they have a drug or alcohol problem, are you helping them? Or are you furnishing their habit? If you continually bail a person out of trouble, will they ever learn the consequence of their actions? The things we have to give are our pearls. Your time is just as valuable as your money, so we must ask ourselves if our time, effort, or money is going to be like casting a pearl or a dollar into a pig's pen. The analogy is that whatever you gave is gone; it is lost in the mud. Once something is gone, you no longer have it to give where there could be benefit to someone. The parables in God's word can be a great tool to help guide a true Christian heart.

Here is an example of a decision many of us are faced with often. (this usually happens at a stop sign). There is a person standing on the side of the road holding a sign. What is the Christian thing to do? Do we turn our head and look away? Do we give them money? Do we dare take them in? Take a second to ask God to show you, and follow your first thought. If it's "no," then consider this: your help could do more harm than good. This is why God gave us the analogy, so that we would not feel guilty and un-Christian by saying no and not casting our pearls before swine. Now if God had said yes when you asked him whether you should help, or if you are still unsure, you could use Peter's example of the lame man at the temple gate asking alms. Peter said silver and gold have I none, such as I have, I give unto you, in the name of Jesus Christ rise up and walk,[26] then he reached out to him. In other words, teach them God's word so God can take care of their needs for the rest of their lives. If you give a hungry man a fish you have fed him for a day, but if you teach him how to fish, you have fed him for a lifetime.

We should be bold enough to stop and ask the person in need if they know who Jesus Christ is. If he is interested, then buy him a meal and while he is eating give of your time and teach him the word. If he is not interested, then reconsider your pearls (cost). I think we all want to walk proud, and confident that we are doing what God wants us to do, not what man wants or thinks we should do. You can't please every man, but you can please God by walking in his word. Men all have different opinions, but God has our answers and his answers will never change. He even said in his word for us to work heartily unto the Lord and not unto men. If you let God's word direct your path and your every decision, then you can walk in peace and confidence.

These parables can also help us to make a confident stand on other things in life when we have a need to. For example, most of us have heard, "Turn the other cheek." How do we know when and with whom we draw the line according to God and still maintain a loving heart? The word says to forgive "seventy times seven,"[27] so obviously there is a limit. There are a number of scriptures from God on this subject, such as, "have no fellowship with them," and "receive him not unto your house," also, "those who have a form of Godliness and deny the power therein, from such turn away," and "Have no fellowship with the unfruitful works of darkness."[28, 29]

"Yet count them not as an enemy," he said, "but that you study to be quiet and to do your own business, walk honestly toward them that are without and you may lack of nothing." If you can help them, help them, but if a person continually takes of your time, and effort, and they are ever learning and never able to come unto a knowledge of the truth, they can be causing distraction from the positives in your own life, and that is the unfruitful works of darkness. God also covered this area for family members, as to where we should draw this same line, when in Luke 8:21 Jesus himself answered and said unto them, "My mother and brethren are they which hear the words of God and do it."[30]

This is God's word telling us that we do not have to be walked on like a doormat because we are Christians. No matter who they are, even family or friends, we do not have to continue being around those who continually harm or hurt us.[31] Eventually, Satan could find a way to destroy us. Also, think about this: there would be no benefit for Satan to destroy those who do his works; he is after those who are walking upright. This is a big key to our understanding of why good people can have many problems or even die at a young age. Satan is watching closely for God's people to slightly miss the mark. The Bible says Satan is come to destroy, but he needs people who will help him do his deeds, and many times he will use one to get to others. Most of the time, the people do not even realize that they are helping Satan. We are to have no fellowship with people who continually bring darkness. Other people may make choices that we would not choose for ourselves, but that does not mean we judge them. Remember, the word says, "Judge not lest ye be judged." "Be quiet and do your own business." "Count them not as an enemy." "Walk honestly toward them." What may be okay for one may not be for others. This is also established in Romans chapter 14. It says in verse 22, "Hast thou faith? Have it to thyself before God. Happy is he that condemn not himself in that thing which he alloweth."[32]

There are so many things in the word for us to draw from, and the perfection of the word allows us to use one verse or all depending on our individual choices. This is because the word cannot contradict itself as long as we understand what it says and never change the message. That same message can give direction on several subjects. If we turn away from a person that brings unfruitful works,[33] God does not condemn us, as long as our hearts are open to receive them back in our lives if they truly repent (change of heart, mind and ways). This is how the word works, and this is the same way God is with us.

We are held accountable for what we know so we have to be very cautious of what we allow in our lives. What others allow in their lives, they are accountable for. The following from God's word shows how our individual understanding and believing are a large factor in the effects from the things we choose. Romans 14:14 says, "I know and am persuaded by the Lord Jesus, that there is nothing unclean of itself but to him that esteemeth any thing to be unclean, to him it is unclean."[34] For meat destroys not the work of God, all things indeed are pure. But it is evil for that man who eateth with offence. Have you faith? Have it to yourself before God. Happy is he that condemns not himself in that which he allows. And he that doubts is damned if he eat it, because he eat not of faith, for whatsoever is not of faith is sin. This same understanding from God answers a million other questions in the world today if you think about it.

Why do some get cancer and not others? Why do some recover and not others? Why do some gain weight and some don't, no matter what they eat? Why do some have high cholesterol from eggs and some don't? Not to mention high blood pressure and heart problems? Again, this document from God, that what we believe and talk about, is what we receive. We are talked into believing at a young age that certain things are hereditary or unhealthy. Studies and science and things we hear knowingly or unknowingly set our believing. Read again the scripture, and he that doubts is damned if he eat it, because he eat not of faith. One way to understand the word "faith," is this: "believe enough to expect." You cannot have faith in any area that you have doubt. Read again scripture reference 32 and 34.

The word also says there is nothing that goes into the man that defiles the man, but that which comes out of the man is what defiles the man. This is not referring to bodily functions. It refers to what you say in your confessions and what your actions are. Actions and confessions are what come out, and they establish your beliefs. This is called the immutability of God's word; what God said cannot change. What we confess and believe is what we get. If we believe things are hereditary, then why not believe that our genes came from Adam or Noah? I wonder, if we set our believing for that, could we live to be eight hundred and still be climbing mountains? What if it's the world that has convinced us that one hundred years old is old? When we understand how to utilize God's word for our direction, we can have a peace in our mind, of approval, that we cannot find in this world. We can also have understanding of the whats and whys in life. Unless we are all likeminded, it's not possible to please every man. God gave us, within his matchless word, the ability to be as individual as we want to be and still know that we have his approval. For he said, "he that in these things serves Christ, is acceptable to God and approved of men." (Romans 14:18)[35]

Scriptures, Chapter 10

1. **1 Corinthians 12:27** Now ye are the body of Christ, and members in particular.

2. **1 Corinthians 12:28** And God hath set some in the church, first apostles, secondarily prophets, thirdly teachers, after that miracles, then gifts of healings, helps, governments, diversities of tongues.

3. **1 Corinthians 12:29** *Are* all apostles? *are* all prophets? *are* all teachers? *are* all workers of miracles?

4. **Hebrews 9:15** And for this cause he is the mediator of the new testament . . .

5. **1 Timothy 2:5** For *there is* one God, and one mediator between God and men, the man Christ Jesus;

6. **Romans 15:4** For whatsoever things were written aforetime were written for our learning,

7. **1 Corinthians 1:2** . . . to them that are sanctified in Christ Jesus called *to be* saints . . .

8. **Hebrews 7:22** By so much was Jesus made a surety of a better testament.

9. **Genesis 2:7** And the Lord God formed man *of* the dust of the ground, and breathed into his nostrils the breath of life; and man became a living soul.

10. **Genesis 2:17** But of the tree of the knowledge of good and evil, thou shalt not eat of it: for in the day that thou eatest there of thou shalt surely die.

11. **Genesis 3:1** . . . Yea, hath God said, Ye shall not eat of every tree of the garden?
12. **Genesis 1:27** so God created man in his *own* image . . .
13. **John 4:24** God *is* a Spirit: and they that worship him must worship *him* in spirit and truth.
14. **Genesis 3:23** Therefore the Lord God sent him forth from the garden of Eden . . .
15. **Genesis 4:1** And Adam knew Eve his wife; and she conceived and bare Cain . . .
16. **John 3:16** For God so loved the world, that he gave his only begotten Son . . .
17. **1 Corinthians 6:20** For ye are bought with a price . . .
18. **1 Corinthians 7:23** Ye are bought with a price; be not ye the servants of men.
19. **Hebrews 9:14** How much more shall the blood of Christ, who through the eternal Spirit offered himself without spot to God, purge your conscience from dead works to serve the living God?
20. **Hebrews 8:6** But now hath he obtained a more excellent ministry, by how much also he is the mediator of a better covenant, which was established upon better promises.
21. **Acts 2:4** And they were all filled with the Holy Ghost, and began to speak with other tongues, as the Spirit gave them utterance.
22. **2 Timothy 3:16** All scripture is given by inspiration of God . . .
23. **Luke 23:43** And Jesus said unto him, Verily I say unto thee, today shall thou be with me in paradise.
24. **Mathew 17:23** . . . and the third day he shall be raised again . . .
25. **Mathew 7:6** Give not that which is holy unto the dogs, neither cast ye your pearls before swine, lest they trample them under their feet, and turn again and rend you.

26. **Acts 3:6** Then Peter said, silver and gold have I none; but such as I have give I thee: In the name of Jesus Christ of Nazareth rise up and walk.

27. **Matthew 18:22** Jesus saith unto him, I say not unto thee, Until seven times: but, Until seventy times seven.

28. **Ephesians 5:11** And have no fellowship with the unfruitful works of darkness, but rather reprove *them*.

29. **2 Corinthians 6:14** Be ye not unequally yoked together with unbelievers: for what fellowship hath righteousness with unrighteousness? And what communion hath light with darkness?

30. **Luke 8:21** And he answered and said unto them, My mother and my brethren are these which hear the word of God and do it.

31. **2 Thessalonians 3:6** Now we command you, brethren, in the name of our Lord Jesus Christ, that ye withdraw yourselves from every brother that walketh disorderly, and not after the tradition which he received of us.

32. **Romans 14:22** Hast thou faith? Have *it* to thyself before God. Happy *is* he that condemneth not himself in that thing which he alloweth.

33. **James 2:14** What *doth it* profit, my brethren, though a man say he hath faith, and have not works?

34. **Romans 14:14** I know, and am persuaded by the Lord Jesus, that *there is* nothing unclean of itself: but to him that esteemeth any thing to be unclean, to him *it is* unclean.

35. **Romans 14:18** For he that in these things serveth Christ *is* acceptable to God, and approved of men.

Chapter 11
How to Walk in the Spirit with God Directing Your Path

Take God's word literally and walk in the deeper truth he intended. I warned you before, this may not be easy at times. The more you pick and choose the scriptures you want to accept and live by, the tougher it's going to be (remember the example of the full armor). The more you choose to live by all of the scriptures, the easier it is. Remember, the word said to live by every word that proceedeth out of the mouth of God. It's the easiest way, according to God, to truly walk in the spirit. Train yourself to look closely, as we did in some of the other examples. Even the smallest things have a deeper truth when seen through spiritual eyes. Then you will see how God really did give us all the answers. Just bring your every thought to the word. Find scriptures to base your stand and don't second-guess it. As long as you understand the message and know it is what God said, it will not change because no other scripture can contradict it. Any other scriptures you can find will only document and establish further. This is living by his every word, not picking and choosing. If you are trying to correct a situation using scripture and you are angered or frustrated then you are picking and choosing. God does not have full power if you are frustrated, because the fruit of the spirit is love, joy, peace, gentleness, etc. We call this having our foot on the hose. This is what cuts to the bottom-line truth, like a two-edged sword, and allows us perfect correction.

God is light and in him there is no darkness; everything is spiritual. It is light or dark, right or wrong, truth or lie. Any way you want to look at it, know for sure that it cannot be both at the same time. Anything that is negative is not from God. Think about this: can light and dark fill the same space? Jesus Christ is your light switch to cast out any darkness from your day. Remember (every knee shall bow), thank him for the positives to cast out quickly the negatives. It is easier to walk with and know God and his word than people have made it out to be.

Believing in Christ puts spirit in us—a spirit seed—and this seed, like others, needs the living water which is the word of God in order to grow. The word says we have fountains of living water,[1] and a fountain has an endless supply and never stops. Spirit food is the only thing that feeds a spirit seed. The more you feed it (spirit food, which is God's word), the bigger and stronger your spirit grows. Once we are born again of that new birth, and we become a spirit person with a perfect connection with God through Christ the mediator, we still have to know what it is that we have, and then we have to know what to do with it, and many people are not being taught this. Therefore many people are born again, but that seed lies dormant and has lack of growth. Remember, Paul planted and Apollos watered.

The word gives us other examples concerning this when it says, "Dost thou understand what thou readest?"[2] And the man said, "How can I, lest some man teach me?" Also, the apostles addressed a group of born-again people, asking them if they had manifested (the manifestations) since they received the Spirit,[3] and the people said they had not heard of it. They were already born again, having heard and believed in Christ, but no one had taught them what was now available to them because of it. So the apostles went on to teach them what to do with it after they had it.

God's word said, ". . . greater is he [Christ] that is in you than he that is in this world,"[4] and Jesus also said, "and greater than these can you do because I go unto my Father."[5] Understanding this spirit and power that is in us is how you utilize the power contained in it for your individual walk.

Learn Satan's devices so we are not blaming God for Satan's actions, and also confusing others, including our children. Even things that seem innocent listen and think about what they are implying. If it is drawing us from the word of truth, don't be fooled, this is how Satan creeps in unaware. The things we do today may seem to be okay, but you could be giving Satan a break in the hedge for weeks or even years from now. Satan was the angel of light, so he can imitate light. You have to always be listening for God, so he can reveal Satan to you, which he does (discerning of Spirits).

Many people are not aware that the inner still voice (their first thought) is from God, therefore most of the time we are not listening. We debate it in our mind and talk ourselves right out of it. Then later want to kick ourselves for not following our first thought. Doesn't God say that we are his children and to cast our cares upon him? And would we, as parents, tell our children if we knew something was going to harm them? God's desire is as ours is with our children, to always help them and save them. Since God has foreknowledge of things, he will often try to warn us. More often than we realize, our first thought is from God. The second thought is our mind, thinking it through with our negative wrong teachings, trying to debate it like our children do with us. God made things easy for us when he placed the spirit of Christ in us, because God, Jesus and the angels are there with us every second to guide and direct our paths, but we have to choose to let them.

His word tells us, "Trust in the Lord with all your heart, lean not unto your own understanding, in all your ways acknowledge him and he shall direct your path."

Truly take some time to consider these truths from God's word to see for yourself. Are these simple truths fitting with exactness in your life? Have you ever been working on something, even something as simple as cutting wood or a tomato when, from out of the blue, a negative thought of cutting yourself comes to you? It may only last a second. You ignore it, and then a split second later you actually cut yourself, or something similar to that flash of a thought happens. Look back on the things that have happened in your life, and consider these patterns. Also, start looking for them in the future; everything I have said is documented in God's word.

Are these things happening in our daily lives? Could God have made life simpler than men are making it out to be? I believe God didn't lie, and that he meant every word he said. Wouldn't these truths make us free from many things, if we believe in them and start listening closer?

How do we know it's God when he talks to us? Bring every thought captive to his word. Satan creeps about like a roaring lion, seeking whom he may devour,[6] so Satan wouldn't be warning you or bringing God's other children to your mind so you would pray for them. We already know God said to trust in him and he will direct you. There is no way anyone (using God's word) can document that these types of things are not available. Also, God did tell us in his word that it is available to understand all mysteries.

Resist the devil and he will flee from you.[7] For every fiery dart, rebuke Satan with the word of truth (a verse from the word) or simply rebuke Satan in the name of Jesus Christ. He is the mediator,[8] which means through Christ you have a perfect connection to God immediately. This is the deeper truth in God's whole plan, because he gives his children, who know and call on his Son, greater and quicker power. That is why Jesus said so many times, "in my name."[9] So in essence, this gives wings to your prayer. The word says that at the name of Jesus Christ every knee shall bow,[10] and he (Jesus) said, whatsoever ye shall ask in my name that I will do, that the Father may be glorified.[11] It was also said: even devils were cast out in the name Jesus Christ. And it was said in Matthew 4:10, in Mark 8:33 and in Luke 4:8 that Jesus Christ said, "get ye behind me Satan." Remember, we can do what he did.

We are also told to stay wise unto that which is good, and simple concerning evil, and the God of peace shall bruise Satan under our feet shortly.

Satan is the god of this world.[12] According to the word, he has power over worldly things, but because of, and through, Jesus Christ, we can choose in every situation to give back to God his authority over us. Remember, God gave us free will, so we choose our path. He has to have permission to intervene and he cannot go against our choices. When a person has chosen to have God direct their life, that does not mean they become perfect. If that person gets out of fellowship for a time, God can still have the ability to protect us. This is why God tells us to pray for others. If this were not the case, he wouldn't need us to pray for others. He would just do what he needed to do. One of the power tools we have is the ability to speak in tongues. This is one of the many areas we can use it. The word says, sometimes you know not what to pray for as you ought. Praying to God in tongues bypasses your mind and Satan cannot creep in or counterfeit it. God's word says that no man speaking by the Spirit calleth Jesus accursed.[13]

God knows all things, but he has to have permission from someone to intervene: if one of his children is out of fellowship (not intentionally, but on the negative, or dark side) and we are without him for a moment—a bad day! Oops. Guess what, God still loves you and he covered this also. If he knows it's not intentional, it does not have to be you. By us speaking or praying to him in tongues he can give himself permission to do things we don't know about. This is in Romans 8:26: the Spirit itself maketh intercession for the saints.[14] God says we have free will. In every thing we do, we can choose to walk with or without him in any situation. Whether we're in or out of fellowship, as soon as we call on him, he is there. He never leaves us; he is just waiting for us to ask for help. These are all immutable laws and free will.[15-17] God said that he gave his angels to have charge over you, but even they have to abide by your free will. So if they know your free-will choice and desire is not to be off track, they can cover things you may not even know about. They cannot choose for you, but they can cover for you if you have let your choice and desires be known to them.

What if God knows one of his children (let's say it's your aunt in Georgia), and God knows she is in trouble or ill. You don't know because it's just happened, but she comes to your mind out of the blue. God can bring her to your mind. "You know not what you should pray for."[18] If you think of her, and speak in tongues, God can cover whatever is needed (intercession).

We have all this power and most people are afraid of it because they don't understand it. This was God's way to help us or save us without breaking his immutable laws. This is established in 1 Corinthians 14:2, "For he that speaketh in an *unknown* [emphasis added] tongue speaketh not unto men, but unto God: for no man understandeth, howbeit in the spirit he speaketh mysteries."[19]

One of the toughest things we have to do is to not back up on the truth. When we don't want to hurt people's feelings or offend them; many times it's not what you say but how you say it. The truth is always what makes people free, and feelings will come and go. No matter what, the truth is still going to be there, and accepting it is the only way to be free, whether it's you or someone else that needs to hear it. Live by every word that proceeds out of the mouth of God and speak it with love and boldness, and be confident in God's promises.

We all know the truth is not always what a person wants to hear—ourselves included. But "the truth will make you free" when you make your stand on God's word. Do not back up on your stand. The truth, when it comes from a loving heart, will make others free as well. You must know for yourself the desires of your heart (the end result you desire) so you are not double-minded,[20] and then give them over to God in the name of Jesus Christ, and it shall be done. You must take into account all of the scriptures and immutable laws that pertain to receiving what you ask for.

If you are not seeing the result, then you are missing at least one of the ingredients, or you simply have not let go and let God. Search his word and you will find your correction. Also remember, most situations we get into don't happen overnight, so they may not get well overnight. So be patient, loving and kind, stay diligent and God will never let you down.

God's word also gives us much direction about receiving reproof and hearing the instruction of the Lord. As it says in Proverbs 1:7, ". . . but fools despise wisdom and instruction."[21] When we are corrected by someone with or according to God's word, it may not be what we want to hear, but remember, the word also says that a wise man receives reproof and will increase in learning, and that it is a wise man who accepts reproof. Think about all things from both sides of a situation at all times, to make sure that you are not the one who needs the correction. Remember that these things in the word apply the same for others as they do for you. If you are heady, high-minded, restless, frustrated or angered, then you are on the negative side, and you cannot receive positives. Read 1 Timothy 6:17, Romans 11:20, and 2 Timothy 3:4.[22-24] You must be correct yourself before you have a right to correct someone else. And consider again, every man is right in his own mind.

Here is a big one: "Fall not into the traditions of men."[25] Or the ninth commandment, "Thou shalt not bear false witness against thy neighbor."[26] Or "put away lying."[27] Every year at Christmas we tell our children that this is to celebrate Jesus Christ's birth and then we tell them this huge, made-up story about this Santa who's coming down the chimney to bring them presents. We continue following these traditions and falling into the commercialism to the point where many even let bills go to cover for the lies. Then years later, tell them we lied about most of the story, but the part about Jesus was true. The truth here is that Satan is winning this silly battle our tradition has brought on us. Think about it. We have taught our children by example that it's okay to tell a lie and at the same time expect them to believe in God and Jesus Christ whom they cannot see. So why not teach them the truth from the beginning of their life? This is no game. God and Jesus Christ and Satan do exist.

We can still celebrate Christmas and we should celebrate Jesus Christ's birth but we should do it in truth. I love the holidays, they are the best time of the year, but I don't believe God wants us to make Santa a bigger part in it than Jesus. We can break away from the traditions without spoiling the season—and quite possibly make them better. Besides, the truth is what makes us free. (What could we be free from in this example: lying, sneaking, cunning, deceiving, etc?)

Here is another truth for those who really want to know how big the truth is. Many people think they know, but are not sure beyond doubt, that Jesus Christ was not born on December 25. Many even know for sure that he wasn't, but they don't teach it as the truth. One reason for this is that there are traditions that we would have to change. But the Bible documents Jesus Christ's birth in Revelation 12 according to the stars and their placement at the time of his birth. The study of this shows that his birth was—get this—September 11th. Some may say that this is one of many different theories based on this same information, but what other date is being taught? And why haven't we Christians agreed on an actual date and time for his birth? Do we not think it is as important as everything else we learn and study? From what I have seen in the word, there are several other things that can confirm this date to you, as you get more familiar with the word. I was shown this ten years ago so it's not something new, but think about how big this is: the date of our saviour, Christ Jesus's birth, is now known as one of the worst days in history. Does Satan know the word better than we do, since he was the angel of light,[28] and is he continually laughing at us and rubbing our faces in it? Are our traditions affecting our so-called Christian walk? If this is truth, then these are the things we need to be teaching our children, not about some Santa who will be gone at the age of six. The word says, train your children up in the nurture and admonition of the Lord and when they are old, they will not depart from it. Should we still be wondering why they are departing from it? Are we living God's truth or our own?[29]

"Raise your children up in the nurture and admonition of the Lord and when they are old they shall not depart from it." How do we do this in today's world? Answer . . . enforce God's laws and directions; he gave us all the answers. If you have God's word in your daily life, walk by every word that proceeds out of the mouth of God no matter what the world tells you. Turn to him and his word and let God direct your path and your children will follow.

I know this sounds too easy, but it can be that easy, and it works. The younger your children are when they learn about God, the easier it is. One of the problems in today's society when it comes to raising our children is the fear of child abuse. It is so obvious that we have allowed this to get out of hand. There is a major difference in correction and abuse and because of the abuse factor many people in this world have fear of correcting their children. Have you ever noticed the looks on people's faces when a child misbehaves in public? They look at the child with disgust. You can see and feel the embarrassment of the parent, and then most panic with doubt, worry and fear about how they should respond. According to the word we have been studying, these are negatives. So what just happened? The adversary (Satan) already won.

The parents don't know what to do; we can't win! Or can we? The Bible says in Ephesians 6:1, "Children, obey your parents in the Lord for this is right,"[30] and it is sad to see how many parents today are obeying their children. As long as we continue looking to the world for answers, this will continue. The world is full of leaders and counselors who continue to come up with new solutions and answers that are obviously not working. They're even making matters much worse. When do we accept that things are worse and that this is a major culprit? Make a stand and tell them we are going back to God's original plan. Isn't this our lives and our children being destroyed?

Like my other life examples in this book, all I have are my own experiences with my children, so I hope I do not sound boastful when I show how wonderful God and his word have worked in this area as well. God and his word will never fail you and the results will prove it every time. My daughter, Ashley, is fourteen and I am so proud of her. Anyone who knows her would say and has said that she is wonderful in every aspect. She is on the honor roll in school and we have not needed to ask her if she did her homework since the first grade. She cleans her room when she knows it needs it, not because we asked her to. She has respect for adults and she would not dream of talking back. I believe these behaviors begin early in life and develop through the years. The only thing I did differently was to follow God's instruction instead of the world's. I would get her attention the first instant she disobeyed. I believe in using only fingers on a little bottom; disciplining without anger was much better and not abusive, the constant battle of authority others were going through. Unlike many others in today's world, fourteen years later I only have honorable stories about my teenager. The following, I believe, is what established this result. I did my best for every negative to give two positives. I would immediately hug her and tell her, "I love you! But it's my job as your mom to teach you to obey me." I even said to her, "Please don't make me have to spank you, because it hurts me to have to do it, and if you misbehave I have to." And she hasn't.

At about age six, she had tested the water and talked back to me. The punishments seemed harsh at the time for a child who was so good, but I let her know, in no uncertain terms, that this was unacceptable. As I recall, my stern words were without anger as I told her, "I will put you through the wall before I will ever allow you to disrespect me or talk back." I gave her two weeks of grounding from everything and we didn't give an inch, even when the county fair came up and all the kids were going. We had to stick to what we said, even though we were grounded as well in order to police it. One week into it I had a hard time sticking to it, but I knew I had to. Still to this day, I have heard her say at times when she sees other children say and do things they shouldn't, "If I did that, my mom would beat me." Which, of course, I have never done, so she probably says this because I have reminded her all her life that she will never get too big for me to do it, if I have to as a last resort.

At times, she has done minor things that she shouldn't, and I have actually sat down with her and talked to her about how important it is for her to listen and obey me the first time I speak. I gave her a few examples such as, "If I don't teach you to hear me, how will you ever know to listen to God?" Also, "What if there was a car coming and you didn't see it? If I have to call you more than once you could be hurt." Our children need to have us explain our reasons for what we do. I have shown her where the Bible says in Ephesians 6:1–4, "Children, obey your parents in the Lord; for this is right. Honor thy father and mother [which is the first commandment with promise];[31] that it may be well with thee, and thou mayest live long on earth." I also explained the following verse, "And, ye fathers provoke not your children to wrath; but bring them up in the nurture and admonition of the Lord."[32] In order for us not to provoke our children, we must not correct or punish them out of anger; that is why he said obey your parents in the Lord. (Remember, we reap what we sow.) Do you want your children to follow you if you are wrong?

The way God is with us is a wonderful example for us to follow; in a loving but firm way, with rules of expectations that do not change, we must communicate and teach them right from wrong, also teaching them that disobedience is not acceptable. No child will be a blessing without guidance and teaching; the same goes for us, as God's children. We need to realize that we are doing our children more harm than good if we allow them to disobey or be disrespectful. If you do not like your own child, who else will? Tell them and show them you love them, even when you have to correct them, and use the word to teach them.

If we understand the accounts in the Bible are how God has instructed us, we can use them for teaching ourselves and our children. One of the accounts from God on this subject you may have heard referred to as "father knows best." This account is in Luke 11:11–12, If a son shall ask bread of any of you that is a father, will you give him a stone? Or if he ask a fish, will you give him a serpent? Or if he shall ask an egg, will you offer him a scorpion?[33] Many of these types of scriptures are related to the eastern world and culture, so in our country and in today's world we overlook the deep analogy. There is so much depth in these types of scriptures if we choose to study for a deeper understanding, but even the surface message, for those who have not been shown their depth, shows the simple analogy. Our message in today's world and in our language could be, if your child asked for a piece of candy, would you give them a pill? The analogy is that if there was a piece of candy and a pill on the table and they are very similar, the child would not know the difference. You would stand firm to protect them, and the parent always knows best. If we do not teach our children to obey our laws or rules how can we expect them to obey God's laws?

Being firm always has its rewards. I know God's laws and expectations for me and I know how much he loves me, so it's easy to have a great love and respect for him, because he never confuses me with new laws or conditions. In following his example, my reward is that Ashley tells me all the time that I am the best mom in the world. She has been a great blessing, just as God promised. For he said, "Correct your children and they shall give you rest."[37] When I was a child I had great respect for my father and I loved him more than anything, and I still do. I also knew my Dad loved me to no end, even though there were many times I thought he was harder on us than he needed to be. No matter what, we always knew if we ever spoke harshly, or started arguing with our parents, we would be knocked out. So he didn't have to do it because we knew the rules wouldn't change. I am not saying that people should start slapping and spanking their children. On the contrary, if they know you will, you won't need to. This is respect, not abuse; there is a big difference between abuse and laying down God's rules for our children and being adamant that they have enough respect that they will want to obey.[35-37] Isn't this the way God is with us? He wants us to obey, and will give us our heart's desires. And at the same time, he expects us to respect him, and do what he tells us to do. Wasn't he the first one to say to his children, "You will reap what you sow"?

For those of you who have older children, even those with problems that may seem out of control or even hopeless, God's word has your answers. If you seek them, you will find them. If you diligently follow God's direction, have God's word in your daily life, walk by every word that proceeds out of the mouth of God no matter what the world tells you—if you turn to him and his word and let them direct your path, your children will follow.

Remember that light dispels darkness in this area as well. When you turn on the light (love, a smile, kind words, etc.) the darkness (attitude, anger, confusion, strife, etc.) has to leave. If you are operating any of these, you will get negative results and so on. This means both of you; this is why he advised the parents not to bring the children unto wrath.

Pray often and talk to God. He will listen, and if you listen, you will hear his answers. You and your children are God's children and his word says, in 3 John 1:4, "I have no greater joy than to hear that my children walk in truth."[38]

The most important thing is that you raise them up in the Lord and when they are old they will not depart from it. And that you put on the whole armor of God. Walk as a soldier, in full armor, knowing who the enemy is and continually teaching your children that they are God's children too. By doing this, they will think to pray for God to protect them and their friends. Teach them to know that when God said "all things," it also includes their school work and tests. Teach them not to limit God in their lives. This is what it means to raise them up in the nurture and admonition of the Lord.

When you teach your children to put God in their mind for their direction, path and strength, they too will come running in with excitement, telling you what God just did for them. This is when you know you are teaching them to know him and that when they are old they will not depart from it.

We are the examples for the children of this day and time. The more they see the power of God working, the more apt they will be to turn to him in their times of need. Ashley and her friend got stuck on a four-wheeler in the woods one time. They struggled with it for quite awhile and finally sat down in defeat. They felt that they had tried everything and Elizabeth said, "Should we pray for it?" Ashley simply said, "Sure" and she began to pray, lifting it to God. When she finished praying she said, "You get on and drive and I will push." As soon as Elizabeth touched the gas, it pulled right off the stump, although Ashley had barely touched it. These girls ran all the way to the house, out of breath to tell us about what God did, and how quickly he had answered their prayer. These are the things we should be seeing and hearing about when people walk with God. God has armed you with everything you need to defeat Satan and to keep you and your children protected. Doubts, worries, frustration and fears are negative, so they allow Satan the ability to manipulate us and our children. Confidence, faith and trust are positive, so these put you in the positive realm, which is where God directs.

When things happen in life, we tend to operate on the negative side of things, but the second we stop trying to do it ourselves and think positively or give God permission to help, even what seems to be a disaster can be resolved in seconds. These are also things that we need to teach our children. Pray for them and do not worry about them. Teach your children God's truth and how to identify Satan's works and they can and will rebuke him, if they are taught to recognize him.

Many are familiar with the account of Job, but it is misunderstood by many. God clearly states in Job 1:8 that Satan was there and he, Satan, was to test and to tempt Job.[39] The reason Satan had a right to do this is stated in what was said in Job 1:5. Job had a fear that his sons had sinned and cursed God in their hearts.[40] Satan cannot get in when there is light, or confidence, faith and trust. But Job had a doubt and a fear, which gave Satan the right to tempt and test him. This is why God could not stop Satan. The word does say that God gave Satan permission in Job 1:12, "And the Lord said unto Satan, Behold, all that he hath is in thy power; only upon himself put not forth thine hand." But the point is not that God gave Satan permission, the point made is *why*. God did not willingly give Job over to Satan for no reason. Job 1:8 says Job was perfect and upright and there was none other like him. What would this example be for us if God chose him to be destroyed? The point is that God could not stop Satan. No matter how righteous we are, if we have fear or doubts Satan still has ability (break in the hedge).

The word of God explains why. Two verses in particular are a big key for our understanding of many other things in the word and in our life and living, and it says in Hebrews 6:17–18 ". . . God willing more abundantly to shew unto the heirs of promise the immutability of his counsel confirmed it by an oath" and, "That by two immutable things, in which it is impossible for God to lie."[16] Immutable means that it cannot be broken or changed. Even God cannot change or go against what he has said and this was the reason God could not stop

Satan. Because God said, believing ye shall receive. That makes it immutable (God's laws even for himself) that whether we believe for good or bad, that is what we will receive. Even people who do not believe in God or his word live by the immutability of believing "ye shall receive." (Note: other laws apply, explained later). This shows the immutability of God's promise. He cannot lie. This is also confirmed in the word when it says the rain falls on the just and the unjust, and at the same time explains why many non-Christians prosper and have health etc., when many Christians don't. If they give, they receive, and they receive what they believe.

But back to Job. Job 3:23, "To a man whose way is hid, and whom God hath hedged in."[41] This verse tells us Job had a hedge of protection around him. His fear had put a break in this hedge of protection that God had around him. God knew he could not stop Satan, as long as Job had fear in his life because of his own immutable laws. So Satan had a right to Job. God knew this and so did Satan; that's why Satan could come before God with such boldness. Look at what Job said in Job 3:25, "For the thing which I greatly feared is come upon me and that which I was afraid of is come unto me."[42] Then in verse 26 Job said, "I was not in safety, neither had I rest, neither was I quiet: yet trouble came."[43] Think about this: when we are worried or have a doubt of something, are we restful or quiet with inner peace? No. That is the example here: doubt, worry or fear are negative believing, the things for us not to do. What we fear or believe is what we get. Job should have trusted that he had raised his children up in the nurture and admonition of the Lord and then simply said, "Thanks, God, for keeping them safe." Then Satan would not have had the right to do him harm.

This is another interesting bit of information from Job that shows the matchless work of God and his word. In Job 1:1–3, God tells us of Job's substance and that he was perfect and upright.[44, 45] And there were born unto him seven sons and three daughters. He referred to Job as the richest man in the East. Through Job's troubles, he had lost all of his seven sons and his three daughters and he had also lost all of his substance. Remember, the italics words were added so if we read without them, in this case it is more understandable. In Job 11:6, "And that he would shew thee the secrets of wisdom, that they are double to that which is! Know therefore that God exacteth of thee than thine iniquity deserveth."[46] God had promised Job back double everything. Look at Job 42:12[47]–13: everything of Job's substance was doubled, but watch God's perfection in verse 13, "He had also seven sons and three daughters."[48] This was the same number he had before, why not fourteen sons and six daughters if God promised double?

Now remember, Job's fear was for his children and he feared that they were not living for God. So by God matching the number of children that Job had previously, it shows the perfection of his word. This reestablishes the return and at the same time, Job was reassured that his children that had died were saved. Wow! What exactness. He will have double in the return. The word of God could not be more perfect. The closer you look, the more you will see.

Everything is spiritual. It's either from God, or it's from the god of this world, who is Satan. This shows again what God meant when he talked about the immutability of his counsel.

In Galatians 5:18, "But if ye be led of the Spirit, ye are not under the law."[49] This is how the ungodly laws of this world are turned away from us. If we are being led by the Spirit, God guides us and protects us with his laws.

There is no way that any one thing can be from both God and Satan at the same time. Even the smallest things in our daily lives are spiritual. What happens when you turn on a light? As soon as the light comes on, the darkness is gone. The darkness has to leave, because (immutability) God said he is light and in him there is no darkness at all. Nothing can be dark and light, good and bad, or right and wrong at the same time. We should be using this every day in every situation, in order to rightly divide the things of this world, as we live them. Ever notice how bad days get worse and good days get better? This is not by chance. And there is no such thing as luck. It is either God who is light, or Satan who is dark, who is involved in every part of a given situation. If our mind is in a positive mode, we will receive positives, and vice versa.

Have you ever wondered why negative people who complain, "woe is me," are always sick, can't work, or can't find a job? It's not the world that's doing this to them, and it's not because they aren't as lucky as some people. It is the negative prince of darkness who is in control because of the immutability of God's word. Anything that is negative will always bring negative results. This again gives more understanding to the phrase, "we reap what we sow." What we plant is what we will get. You cannot grow grapes from a watermelon seed (the same immutability); God's word has laws that cannot change.

This is pretty simple when we bring everything to the word for understanding. If you have negatives in your life, you can change this pattern by thinking positive thoughts about everything, and thanking God for the perfect outcome. When you catch yourself saying something negative, immediately change it back to a positive.

This is how positive people get positive results. Positive people don't have time to get sick, and don't get sick very often. The reason they don't get sick is not by chance or luck, it is the positive mindset. A positive person does not give in as easily when Satan throws fiery darts at them. When they do get into a negative frame of mind, it gives Satan operating space and negative things happen for them as well, but only until they turn to God, or simply change their mind.

Positive people know they cannot be down for long, so they establish a plan, set their minds, and expect positive results. Once again showing the truth in the immutability of the God's word: believing ye shall receive, we reap what we sow and at the same time confirm that a double-minded man is unstable in all his ways.

Stop for a moment and think about this immutability of God's word and how much understanding of worldly issues this gives us. Also consider it from another aspect. When I was growing up, some of my family members were very superstitious. If a bird flew into a window and died, someone was going to die. If an umbrella was opened in the house, three family members would die. If you walked under a ladder, you were going to be injured. If you broke a mirror, you would have seven years bad luck. I have heard them all. I remember that when I was a child, a man from the studio came to our house to take family portraits. My mother was frantic when he opened an umbrella for one of my sister's photos. She knew three family members were going to die. Within three months we lost my grandpa and two of her aunts.

One time when I was older and had my own home, I was on the phone with my mother when a bird flew into my kitchen window and died. She was all upset and I told her that nothing was going to happen, and it didn't. These kinds of things made sense to me for the first time in my life when I first came to God's word and considered the possibility that what we believe or confess is what we receive. When a person does not believe in something, then it won't happen.

I also considered this: what about the ones who do believe in the superstition and they knock on wood, why do the things not happen? Because they knocked on the wood, they now believe it will not happen. So the law of positive believing overrides the negative, like light overrides darkness. When you turn on a light, the dark cannot stay. The same principle applies. Negatives cannot stay in a positive mind. To sum it up, they give the credit to the wood and not God, like Samson did with his hair, because in their minds they believed that knocking on wood was what made it not happen. No matter what it takes to set our mind, we receive that belief. I believe God and his word are much bigger than we give him credit for.

Satan is the prince of the power of the air.[50] Internet, televisions, radio, everything gives off something. Sure, it should be easy to say, if it's bad or ugly or non-truth, turn it off. But how realistic is that, in this day and time? So what can we do as Christians, since Satan is creeping in unawares in more ways than we know? The sad part is, I think most of us see it but we don't know what to do about it without being the un-liked family member. Can you imagine your family's response to you if you took out everything that comes over the air and you tell them it's from Satan so they can't watch or listen to it?

Here is one thing we can do. Learn Satan's devices; point him out to people when we recognize him and his works. One of his biggest devices is keeping people from acknowledging him, and the fact that he does exist, so he is very subtle. This is why people are not rebuking him. Satan does not have power over us unless we allow him to. Satan is bold and he actually uses his own names most of the time. But he has put other names in this world by planting little seeds, so his names are as common as Santa and elves and Mother Nature. They do not exist, but their names are as common as his.

Showing violence and crime on television is another of Satan's greatest tools. We adults and our children are so accustomed to seeing blood, death and negatives that it is not uncommon or as uncomfortable as it used to be for us to see it, or do it in real life. Television does not have to be just Satan's tool; we can use it as our tool if we teach awareness of Satan as much as we teach about God to our children, and use the television as visual examples of Satan's work. Then, point out God's work when he prevails in the end. Most of what we see on television is happening in the world outside. Notice how those horror movies have become our common news. Satan is teaching people how to do these evil things on our own televisions, computers and radios. Satan is creeping in unawares, so in order to defeat him, bring everything captive to the word of God and don't be afraid to say it or to use it.

Television is not all bad; it depends on how we use it. Some programs can be a prime example of God's word and promises evidenced in our life, and can show visuals of love and giving, and can be an inspiration to many. We can use the programs on television to see and teach ourselves and others, including our children, about God and his promises.

Walk in the truth from God's word and nothing but his word, by searching God and his scripture, even if you just use the ones I have shared with you. Make your stand and don't let anyone talk you out of it; this alone will change your life more than you may think.

When you look at even the little things in the world through spiritual eyes, you will see the perfection of God's word, and you cannot prove it wrong. Even things like the weather are under these same immutable laws that we are under. Mother Nature is non-existent, but she gets blamed for a lot of Satan's actions, like storms and bad weather. I have also heard people say, they are an act of God.

Don't storms cause darkness? They steal, kill, and destroy, and they come by way of air. That is Satan's works, according to God. Remember, Jesus simply said peace be still, oh ye of little faith. So while people are blaming Mother Nature, Satan is getting away with it. God or Mother Nature are taking the blame, when all we would have to do is say, "peace be still" and have faith, in order to stop the storm. Consider again all things, whatsoever you ask, in the name of Jesus Christ it shall be given unto you. This is the reason God put all his examples and accounts in his word. Most of us know these accounts. We are just not using them in our lives.

There are immutable laws in the word that we need to consider when utilizing the power we have been given. For example, think about this: there are hundreds of skiers who want it to snow, or people who make a living driving a snow plow. If they are praying or believing for snow, the immutable laws work for them as well. What they ask for, and believe, is what they receive. We must know God's word very well in order to know what is available and how to receive what we need. If your believing and need is big enough, God has promised that he will give whatsoever you ask in the name of his Son. Although he cannot break his immutable laws, we are not limited in having our individual need covered. This is why it is so important for us to know and understand his word; it's the only way to evidence the promises. God did not lie or make idle promises. God did his part and he told us to be doers of the word, and not hearers only.

When you were told you could drive, that did not make you a driver. You still had to be a doer by learning the rules and laws, and then you practiced—driving cautiously and learning by your mistakes. As it says in Malachi 3:10, "prove me now herewith saith the Lord of hosts, if I will not open the windows of heaven, and pour you out a blessing, that there shall not be room enough to receive it."[51] We can all learn to utilize the power of God that Christ had, and recognize what comes from Satan.

We all know storms do bring darkness; they steal from us by the damage they do, they kill people, and they often destroy everything in their path. How much clearer and perfect could God have been in his instructions to us? He even advised us to live one day at a time. He even told us the weather one day at time. In Matthew 16:2–3, "He answered and said unto them when it is evening, ye say it will be fair weather for the sky is red. And in the morning, it will be foul weather today for the sky is red."[52] This is where the phrase came from: red sky at night, sailor's delight, red sky at morning, sailors take warning. But people have chosen to have the weatherman tell us a week in advance.

Now how does this fit with the law of believing? Our weather could now depend on how many watched and believed or talked about the weather report. If enough of us do not listen and believe the negative things, where would we be? Is it possible we are our own worst enemy? I believe Satan is our enemy and he is keeping us blind to God's simple design. I cannot begin to tell you how many times our family and friends have prayed and stopped the rain or storms when there has been need. There is no such thing as luck or chance; everything can be explained by God's perfect word, but only if a man of God wants to see it. Because the word does tell us that the natural man receives not the things of the Spirit of God for they are foolishness unto him, neither can he know them for they are spiritually discerned.

Think about this: people watch the weather report and it sets their believing to what the weatherman said. Then that becomes what people are talking about and believing for. Think about this: if we believe God's word—and he said many times, all things whatsoever you shall ask, believing you shall receive—and God cannot lie, aren't we getting what we ask and believe for? Also, how can God not stop the rain or storm if you or I ask and believe for it in the name of Jesus Christ? If God's word is true, the believing of the people is the determining factor in many cases as to the weatherman being right or not. We, as believers in God and his word, could change these patterns in our lives, if we believe this is truth and we understand how it works.

Remember, God says, "All things whatsoever we shall ask, believing, we shall receive." He never said except for the weather. He said all things whatsoever.

We have been given the control; we just don't know to use it. The following are just four of many scriptures that document that this is available. "Greater is he that is in you than he that is in the world," is one. Also, "That if two of you shall agree on earth as touching anything that they shall ask, it shall be done for them of my Father which is in heaven."[53] And, "all things, whatsoever ye shall ask in prayer, believing, ye receive."[54] If we all teach the same truth, the truth shall make us all free, and don't forget, Jesus calmed the storm by saying, "Peace, be still."[55, 56] and he said, "Oh ye of little faith." And he said in John 14:12, "He that believeth on me, the works that I do, shall he do also."[5]

We can "do all things through Christ" if we do what the word says, and change these patterns we have developed by following

Ephesians 4:22, "Put off the former conversation and put on the new man." A word to the wise: Satan cannot hear your thoughts, he can only go by your actions and expressions, or what you say out loud. He loves it when we limit God.

Scriptures, Chapter 11

1. **Jeremiah 17:13** . . . the fountain of living waters . . .
2. **Acts 8:30** . . . Understandest thou what thou readest?
3. **Acts 8:14** Now when the apostles which were at Jerusalem heard that Samaria had received the word of God.
4. **1 John 4:4** . . . greater is he that is in you than he that is in this world.
5. **John 14:12** He that believeth on me, the works that I do shall he do also; and greater *works* than these shall he do; because I go unto my Father.
6. **1 Peter 5:8** Be sober, be vigilant; because your adversary the devil, as a roaring lion, walketh about, seeking whom he may devour . . .
7. **James 4:7** . . . Resist the devil and he will flee from you.
8. **1 Timothy 2:5** For *there is* one God, and one mediator between God and men, the man Christ Jesus.
9. **Matthew 7:22** . . . and in thy name have cast out devils? and in thy name many wonderful works?
10. **Philippians 2:10** That at the name of Jesus every knee should bow.
11. **John 14:13** And whatsoever ye shall ask in my name, that will I do, that the Father may be glorified in the Son.
12. **2 Corinthians 4:4** In whom the god of this world hath blinded the minds of them which believe not, lest the light of the glorious gospel of Christ, who is the image of God, should shine unto them . . .
13. **1 Corinthians 12:3** Wherefore I give you to understand, that no man speaking by the Spirit of God calleth Jesus accursed:

14. **Romans 8:26** . . . the Spirit itself maketh intercession for us . . .
15. **Hebrews 6:17** Wherein God, willing more abundantly to shew unto the heirs of promise the immutability of his counsel confirmed *it* by an oath . . .
16. **Hebrews 6:18** That by the two immutable things, in which *it was* impossible for God to lie . . .
17. **Ezra 7:13** . . . which are minded of their own free will.
18. **Romans 8:26** Likewise the Sprit also helpeth our infirmities: for we know not what we should pray for as we ought . . .
19. **1 Corinthians 14:2** For he that speaketh in an *unknown* tongue speaketh not unto men, but unto God: for no man understandeth *him;* howbeit in the spirit he speaketh mysteries.
20. **James 1:8** A double-minded man *is* unstable in all his ways.
21. **Proverbs 1:7** . . . *but* fools despise wisdom and instruction.
22. **1 Timothy 6:17** Charge them that are rich in this world, that they be not highminded, nor trust in uncertain riches, but in the living God, who giveth us richly all thing to enjoy . . .
23. **Romans 11:20** Well; because of unbelief they were broken off, and thou standest by faith. Be not highminded, but fear . . .
24. **2 Timothy 3:5** Having a form of godliness, but denying the power thereof: from such turn away.
25. **Mathew 15:3** . . .Why do ye also transgress the commandment of God by your tradition?
26. **Deuteronomy 5:20** Neither shalt thou bear false witness against thy neighbor . . .
27. **Proverbs 30:8** Remove far from me vanity and lies . . .
28. **2 Corinthians 11:14** And no marvel; for Satan himself is transformed into an angel of light.
29. **Colossians 2:8** Beware lest any man spoil you through philosophy and vain deceit, after the tradition of men . . .
30. **Ephesians 6:1** Children, obey your parents in the Lord for this is right . . .

31. **Ephesians 6:2** Honour thy father and mother; which is the first commandment with promise . . .
32. **Ephesians 6:4** And, ye fathers, provoke not your children to wrath: but bring them up in the nurture and admonition of the Lord . . .
33. **Luke 11:11** If a son shall ask bread of any of you that is a father, will he give him a stone? Or if *he ask* a fish, will he for a fish give him a serpent?
34. **Luke 11:12** Or if he shall ask an egg, will he offer him a scorpion?
35. **Jeremiah 2:30** In vain have I smitten your children; they received no correction: your own sword hath devoured your prophets, like a destroying lion.
36. **Proverbs 23:13** Withhold not correction from the child . . .
37. **Proverbs 29:17** Correct thy son, and he shall give thee rest . . . .
38. **3 John 1:4** I have no greater joy than to hear that my children walk in truth.
39. **Job 1:8** And the Lord said unto Satan, Hast thou considered my servant Job, that *there is* none like him in the earth . . .
40. **Job 1:5** . . . for Job said, it may be that my sons have sinned, and cursed God in their hearts . . .
41. **Job 3:23** . . . to a man whose way is hid, and whom God hath hedged in?
42. **Job 3:25** For the thing which I greatly feared is come upon me, and that which I was afraid of is come unto me.
43. **Job 3:26** I was not in safety, neither had I rest, neither was I quiet; yet trouble came.
44. **Job 1:1** There was a man in the land of Uz, whose name was Job; and that man was perfect and upright, and one that feared God, and eschewed evil.
45. **Job 1:2** And there were born unto him seven sons and three daughters.

46. **Job 11:6** And that he would shew thee the secrets of wisdom, that *they are* double to that which is! Know therefore that God exacteth of thee *less* than thine iniquity *deserveth*.

47. **Job 42:12** So the Lord blessed the latter end of Job more than his beginning . . .

48. **Job 42:13** He had also seven sons and three daughters.

49. **Galatians 5:18** But if ye be led of the Spirit, ye are not under the law.

50. **Ephesians 2:2** Wherein in time past ye walked according to the course of this world, according to the prince of the power of the air, the spirit that now worketh in the children of disobedience . . .

51. **Malachi 3:10** Bring ye all the tithes into the storehouse, that there may be meat in mine house, and prove me now herewith, saith the Lord of hosts, if I will not open you the windows of heaven, and pour you out a blessing, that *there shall* not *be room* enough *to receive it*.

52. **Matthew 16:2-3** He answered and said unto them, When it is evening, ye say, *It will be* fair weather: for the sky is red. And in the morning, *it will be* foul weather to day, for the sky is red and lowering.

53. **Matthew 18:19** . . .That if two of you shall agree on earth as touching anything that they shall ask, it shall be done for them of my Father which is in heaven . . .

54. **Mathew 21:22** and all things, whatsoever you shall ask in prayer, believing, ye shall receive.

55. **Psalms 107:29** He maketh the storm a calm, so that the waves thereof are still.

56. **Matthew 8:26** . . .Why are ye fearful, O ye of little faith? Then he arose, and rebuked the winds and said unto the sea; And there was a great calm.

Chapter 12
Do We Know How Often We Limit God?

When I first learned about praying, I took my daughter to her grandma's for the day because she wanted to spend time with her cousin while I went to work. As I walked across the yard to my car, I prayed for God to protect the girls and to watch over them. I prayed a long and specific prayer. Hours later, I had a phone call that my nephew was at Grandma's and had swallowed some of her blood pressure pills and he was in the ER. On the way to pick up my daughter, I wondered how this could have happened because I knew that I had prayed for the children. No! I had prayed for the girls, not knowing the boy would be there later. Then I began questioning why and how Satan had done this. Well, I told him how he could get in for one, by saying "the girls" out loud in my prayer. Satan's main goal at that moment was not to hurt the boy. His goal was to steal my believing, by trying to cause me to doubt God or unconsciously lose my confidence in prayer.

I sure learned about limiting God. I had tied his hands and taken away his permission to watch over the boy, all in the same prayer. I may have left doors open unaware, but when I searched God's word to find out why, I was no longer ignorant about being cautious when I pray. Our negative confessions or actions are what Satan seeks the most. So whether the issue we deal with is health, finance, marriage, children or even the weather, our lack of application of God's simple direction is what allows Satan the ability to devour, or steal, the word from us.

Another example of the consequences when we limit God appeared when Ashley was about three. We had been teaching her to pray for things, and even when she would get a tiny bump or scratch, we would pray for her. She would forget all about it and go back to playing. One day, I was sitting with my foot soaking in a bucket of hot salt water. I had stepped on a rusty nail a few days before that, and it had become extremely infected. It was so bad that I thought it was going to turn green, and I remember thinking I would probably even need to get a tetanus shot. When Ashley came in from playing outside, she asked me, "What are you doing Mommy?" I told her, and she asked me if she could see it. When I showed it to her, she said, "Do you want me to pray for you?" What was I going to say other than, "Sure!" She prayed for me—a loving prayer without hesitation, kissed me, and went back out to play. As I sat, still in doubt, with my foot back in the bucket, I realized that my believing was not going to allow God and Ashley's prayer to work. I remembered that even Jesus had to remove the unbelievers out of the way. I thought about Ashley's simple believing, and that if my toe was not to heal, it could cause her to doubt prayers. So I prayed to God for him to cover for my believing. I emptied the water, started cleaning the house, and forgot about it. The next morning, Ashley reminded me of it as soon as she woke up. In her sleepy little voice, she asked, "How is your toe, Mommy?" When I said, "Fine," she asked, "Can I see it?" With a slight hesitancy, I lifted my foot, and neither of us could see even a trace of the injury.

It's easier to have simple believing as a child. The older we get, the more old-man habits we have to reckon dead, and the harder it is to put on the new man. This is why God said to "come unto him as a child." God wants us to prosper and be in health. So he can, and will, cover for us, even when our believing gets in his way. The toughest part when first learning this true depth from God's word is that we have to renew our minds, and put on the new man daily, and break those old habits.

Signs, miracles and wonders follow those who believe. The more you look and ask God for these things, the more you will see them and have them. Even the tiniest things are available to you from God. It takes no more effort for God to move a mountain or raise someone from the dead than it does for him to give you a front row parking spot or move the clouds for you. All things whatsoever you shall ask, believe and ye shall have it. If you ask God, he will even give you a visual sign to tell you your prayer has been answered, and sometimes we need to see something visual to help us to believe for it. God is a very personal Father to you and he will work with you on your level. Just like we do with our children, what God does for you is based on your relationship with him, and what you ask him for.

I love to look at the stars in the sky at night. When I go in the hot tub on a cloudy night, I remind God how much I love to see his stars, and thank him for them. He instantly moves back the clouds. My family has witnessed things like this often. We have literally watched the clouds open up directly over our head and continue opening out to a large circle of starry sky just over our five acres. God will give you whatsoever you need, want and ask for, as long as it does not go against his word.

Ashley and I have had several occasions during times of traveling when we had need for God to work his wonders, and he has never let us down. One time I was driving home from Atlanta, Georgia to Michigan. It was in the winter, and I had been driving all night. As we were coming through Cincinnati, Ohio, I was getting pretty tired and suddenly, there was a really bad storm. I could hardly see through the snow and there were vehicles of every kind sliding, crashing and hitting walls, flipping and landing upside down all around us. The road was so slick I dared not try to stop, even to help. While calling 911, I was finally able to slow down to nearly a crawl.

As we continued driving, there were vehicles off the road every quarter mile. We then realized that we hadn't prayed yet. When we began to pray, immediately there was a rest area exit. As we drove off the ramp, I called my husband and told him the roads were too bad to continue and I was going to get some rest.

With such a short distance left to travel, I became restless and I called Bob back and said, "Pray for us, we're firing up this bird and flying home." Ashley and I prayed again but this time it was for the roads to be clear and for a safe trip home. As we drove out of the parking lot to re-enter the highway, the snow had completely disappeared and the road was actually dry. There was not a trace of the storm or any other vehicles in distress, and all this had happened within a maximum of twenty minutes. The rest of the trip, the weather was beautiful.

Another time, we couldn't see the car in front of us and I was about to pull over when I called Bob. He said he would pray for us.

As soon as I hung up the phone, the road was clear and the storm was on both sides of the highway and behind us. This pattern followed us all the way home. Every turn we made, the storm was on both sides of us and behind us. When we got to our house, the storm was at the end of the street just past the driveway.

There was also a time when my sister and I were traveling with two cars. I was following her and the road conditions were so bad that we decided to pull over and get a hotel room. When we pulled off at the exit, there was no hotel. We took a moment, prayed about the weather, and drove straight back up the on-ramp, and back onto a clear highway.

These kinds of things don't happen by chance; they happen far too perfectly and instantly. God's word tells us, "we have not because we ask not." Most of us will wait until we are desperate and then ask, but even then God will not let us down. The instant we ask, we have. It's usually that old-man nature (our old habits), which God tells us we need to reckon dead, that are keeping us from simply asking. God's power is unlimited, it just gets slowed down or detoured, going around us.

When you expect God to answer you, he will, and you will see it. But if you are not looking for spiritual things, you cannot see them. But, if you ask—seeking God with your whole heart—he will give it. Even when you have questions about things that are going on, God can show you signs, to guide you.

There was a time last year that God showed Ashley and me a vision, using the clouds to answer a question I had asked him. I had bought a horse and was boarding him at a nearby farm. Things were fine for a while, and one day a woman showed up with a stallion to board there. This horse seemed very threatening—almost spooky. I did not trust him, and things seemed awkward and uncomfortable from the moment he arrived. A few days later, I met the woman who owned the horse and I knew something was not right, but I wasn't quite sure what.

Early that evening, I sat in the hot tub with Ashley. She had no idea that I had been asking God to show me what was going on. Almost instantly, a puffy white cloud came over the top of the house and I told Ashley to look at it. She said, "Wow, it's a woman riding a horse." We watched as this cloud remained in perfect form until it disappeared over the trees. A second later, Ashley said, "Mom look at that one. Whatever it is, it looks really evil." God had confirmed to me that there were evil spirits connected with them.

The next day, I was feeding the horses in the barn and this horse acted like he was spooked. He literally went mad in the stall. I remember thinking that if he got out, he would absolutely kill me. I immediately said, "Stop it, in the name of Jesus Christ," and he calmed right down and turned his face from me in the stall. The next day the woman took the horse to board him elsewhere; no one ever said why. But I knew God had taken care of it.

Knowing that this is available comes from knowing the examples in the word that document that animals can have devil spirits in them. The word says that every knee shall bow; also, in the beginning, Adam was given charge, even over the animals. We can even demand a bee or a pesky fly to flee from us in the name of Jesus Christ. If we believe, they have to flee. My family has seen proof of things like this for years.

What we do for God doesn't even come close to what God does, or has done, for us. Since I began bringing everything to God's word for understanding, I think the greatest lesson I have learned and now understand on this subject is this: The more we seek to find God, live right or fix the errors in our lives, the craftier Satan will be to stop us, or try to distract us. So we may not always be able to stop Satan from trying, but with God and his word, we can stop him from succeeding in whatever he's up to.

Whether your issues are in marriage, raising children, health, finance, a gambling problem, drugs now and then, or a major drug addiction, God's word has your doctrine. If you accept his reproof, you can be free. God and I also walked away clean from drugs, years ago, and we never looked back. So all these things I speak of, I speak from personal experience. I have tested and watched God's word work with exactness for nearly twelve years, and could never once prove it wrong. God's word is as true, perfect, deep and simple, or as complicated, as we choose to make it. We each have a personal and individual walk with our Father and his word. Just be cautious as you walk. He said trust in him, stay wise in that which is good, and simple concerning evil, but remember he said first you must trust him.

I certainly considered hiding out before I began writing, like Jonah and Noah did, especially when it came to putting all this in a book to share with you. Many of the experiences I have to share with you are because Satan does exist and he knows and sees things too. I'm sure my heart's desires have been a threat to Satan, and I know he does not want us to succeed, because my greatest hope and desire of all is that all of us will share the joys, peace and rewards we'll have in heaven, and to bring more of them to Earth while we wait.

You can choose to believe that these things I have written are true, or you can think they are silly; the choice is up to you. I learned a long time ago that it's not what man thinks, but what God knows, and what my heart tells me. Besides, what are the options? Doubt, worry, fear, confusion! What do we have to lose? These things I speak are told to us from God's word, which we all read. They are not my opinions. I just choose to believe what he has said and I have proven and tested them in my life and cannot prove them wrong.

Therefore I can speak with boldness that God is not the author of confusion and he did not say things to confuse us or to lose us. On the contrary, he said that his people are being destroyed for a lack of knowledge.

The same scriptures and promises throughout this book have applied to, and documented, everything I have written in this chapter as well, so they are not repeated on a scripture page. How many times do we need to read them before we believe them, and go to the bank?

From the minor to the major things in life, how often are we limiting God?

Read the following scriptures for added encouragement.

Scriptures, Chapter 12

1. **James 5:14** Is any sick among you? Let him call for the elders of the church; and let them pray over him, anointing him with oil in the name of the Lord . . .

2. **James 5:15** And the prayer of faith shall save the sick, and the Lord shall raise him up; and if he have committed sins, they shall be forgiven him.

3. **James 5:16** Confess *your* faults one to another, and pray one for another, that ye may be healed. The effectual fervent prayer of a righteous man availeth [makes available] much.

4. **James 4:2** Ye lust, and have not: ye kill, and desire to have, and cannot obtain: ye fight and war, yet ye have not, because ye ask not.

5. **James 4:3** Ye ask, and ye receive not, because ye ask amiss, that ye may consume *it* upon your lusts.

6. **James 1:4** . . . that ye may be perfect and entire, wanting nothing.

7. **James 1:5** If any of you lack wisdom, let him ask of God, that giveth to all *men* liberally, and upbraideth not: and it shall be given him.

8. **James 1:6** But let him ask in faith, nothing wavering. For he that wavereth is like a wave of the sea driven with the wind and tossed.

9. **2 Peter 3:15** . . . even as our beloved brother Paul also according to the wisdom given unto him hath written unto you.

10. **1 John 3:22** And whatsoever we ask, we receive of him, because we keep his commandments, and do those things that are pleasing in his sight.

11. **1 John 5:14** And this is the confidence that we have in him, that if we ask any thing according to his will, he heareth us . . . .

12. **1 John 5:15** And if we know that he hear us, whatsoever we ask, we know that we have the petitions that we desired of him.

13. **Romans 8:37** Nay, in all these things we are more than conquerors through him that loved us.

14. **1 Corinthians 2:14** But the natural man receiveth not the things of the Spirit of God: for they are foolishness unto him: neither can he know *them*, because they are spiritually discerned.

15. **Mark 11:24** Therefore I say unto you, What things soever ye desire, when ye pray, believe that ye receive *them*, and ye shall have *them*.

16. **1 John 5:13** These things have I written unto you that believe on the name of the Son of God; that ye may know that ye have eternal life, and that ye may believe on the name of the Son of God.
17. **2 Corinthians 2:11** Lest Satan should get an advantage of us: for we are not ignorant of his devices.

Chapter 13
But . . . Don't We all Need Money?

God's word says, "The love of money is the root of all evil."[1] Notice he did not say money is the root of all evil, but that the love of money is. The word also says that God knows your needs, so we must ask, is money a want for us or do we need money? If we are to live the more-than-abundant life that he talked about in his word,[2] of course we need money! The word does not just say "abundant," God's desire for us is more than abundant, that we might have through Christ.[3] Abundant means the bills are paid; more than abundant means that after the bills are paid our wants and desires are also covered. God wants us to have all those things that make us happy and comfortable. God also said we are to be examples to others. Who would want what we have if we are not prospering and in health?[4] So I ask you, is it wrong to ask God for money? Of course not! So, if you are not prospering, it could be as simple as God's immutable laws. They apply in this area the same as others; remember they cannot be broken. What you believe for and ask for you will receive. The biggest law that applies regarding money or personal things, according to the word, is that we don't love or desire them more or put them above God and giving. When you give, you receive; it's an immutable law.

So give from your heart, for this is what God looks upon. You are to trust in him to supply your every need, and he will give you the desires of your heart according to his riches and glory,[5] which is, according to his word, above and beyond all that we may ask or think. Many times we are informed through figures of speech what is available, so we must learn to read and understand the message. We find one of these in Psalm 50:10, "For every beast of the forest is mine, and the cattle upon a thousand hills."[6] Verse 14 says, "Offer unto God thanksgiving; and pay thy vows unto the most high."[7] Verse 15 goes on, "and call upon me in the day of trouble: I will deliver thee, and thou shalt glorify me."[8]

So be thankful to him for all that you have and when you have a need, call upon him and place your troubles on him. He will give you as many cattle as you need, because he said they are already yours. Even cattle have value, right? Consider Job for a moment, a man of God, richest man in the East. God himself gave him back double because he stayed faithful. There is another immutable law that could apply when we are in financial trouble. In James 1:8 God's word warns us, "A double-minded man is unstable in all his ways."[9]

Until you choose a direction, you are double-minded, and this makes you unstable in all your ways. Until you set an amount to cover all your needs and set your believing for the full fix, God is limited because you are unstable and on the negative side of the immutable laws. Also, if you have a partner that is not likeminded with you, your finances could be unstable. But if you sit down and make a decision together, and set an amount, then you must agree to a path of correction. The word says that where two agree as touching any one thing it shall be done.[10] The word also says that, "where two or more are gathered together in my name, there I am in the midst of them."[11] Don't forget the rest of the immutable laws we have seen in God's word. They all apply to every little thing and they will not ever change or contradict each other. You must search his word, to know what's available, and then you will find answers for receiving it.

Continue to have God and his word first in your every thought because, like Job, God's word holds your answers for keeping it. God gave his children promises in a cup that runs over; the silver spoon is optional.

"Ye shall offer a tenth of the tithe," has become a thorn in the flesh of many people. Satan has turned it into a vicious circle; it is the key ingredient to receiving from God, "the more than abundant life," when it is properly operated.

I have spoken to many people who have a negative opinion of giving tithes to the church for many reasons. I myself have understood many of their views because they are legitimate from their perspective. This is because there is lack of understanding of tithing according to God; let's look at what God's true meaning of tithing is and how it works.

Again we need to consider the immutable laws of God; they cannot change or be broken. When you give, you receive. The key to having is giving, because God promises back one hundredfold of what you give. The catch is that it has to come from the heart. The heart is being taken out of the giving when it becomes a dollar amount that we don't think we can afford. Then it can become a small pressure point, which is a negative for the person giving. This gives Satan room to hold them back because of the doubt, worry or fear that comes from not understanding when and how will it come back as promised. If you do not fully understand something, can you be confident? No.

So what side are you on if the opposite of confidence is doubt? You cannot get positives from negatives. If you are in doubt, you are on the negative side of the immutable law. You will receive the negatives, and you cannot receive the hundredfold. To simplify this, "what you believe is what you will receive," and this applies to every thing in your life, not just tithing.

I have read the context of these messages from God concerning tithing in eighteen scriptures,[12-15] I will list them at the end of this chapter for you to look up and read. Be sure to read the context before and after, because not one of them refers to money. They tithe of what they have: wheat, seed, fruit, and of their herds and flocks.

People do not fully understand this subject, and it has been wrongly taught and used for the benefit of the church in many cases. I don't believe this is the intent of the churches, but it is the result from the deviation of God's perfect design. Therefore Satan has been able to water down the benefits of tithing, and it has become a burden instead of the benefit and blessing it was intended to be. Many people are seeing the churches prospering, and leave there still having to deal with the lack of abundance in their own lives. But the worst part is they still lack the understanding of how to correct these issues in their lives, which is mostly caused from the lack of teaching from that same church. This is part of the vicious circle. Far too many of God's children are living paycheck to paycheck. Some can't even afford to go to church because of embarrassment due to the lack of tithe they feel they can give, while others have to work instead of going to service. Some of those same people are filing for bankruptcy and still tithing, waiting for the return, and they don't understand what they are doing wrong. Are the churches above tithing? Peter was the example of this when he said, "silver and gold have I none, but such as I have I give unto you, in the name of Jesus Christ of Nazareth rise up and walk."[16] This is not just a physical walk. We are to teach people the word so they can rise up and walk.

There is never recorded in the Bible a time when Jesus Christ or the apostles ever passed the horn or the plate, and they always had plenty. It wasn't just money that they needed. Those who had food would feed them, and those who had herds would give them a donkey for traveling. People were willing to give them a place to stay because they were blessed to hear them speak the wonderful works of God.

How would this work in our world? Those who have money give it from the heart. If you own a car dealership, give the teacher a car, one hundredfold means you will sell one hundred more than you would have, had you not given the one. Give from the heart and believe, and trust God to supply all your riches according to his riches and glory. If you sew, make the linens for the church. Carpenters could build it. If you have time, give it, and so on. This was the intent of the tithe in God's original plan. Look it up. Give freely of what you have to give; the more you give, the more you will receive.

Don't think this means you should not tithe. On the contrary, this means that you should give money to the church. If they are teaching you the true word of God, you should give to them from the heart. The teachers are no different than you are. As men of God, they deserve the same abundant life God gives you. The truth is that if they spend their time studying God's word, so they can teach you after you get done working at your job, then they are doing their job and they need to have money to live and support their families. They also need and deserve, as a child of God, a nice dependable car so they can come to you when you are in need. This is truth and logic.

The problem comes from the church thinking that they need a bigger, nicer building to bring in more people for the tithe, when many are not even meeting the needs of the people that they have. They are leaving so many people lost, searching and wondering, so what is wrong?

Imagine the response of the pastor of your church and the people around you if you put a ham in the plate—that's what is wrong. Many churches have made it the love of money and that is the root of all evil.

When was the last time you heard a minister say, "One of our members has gotten in a jam, so we are passing the plate for him today. Please give what you can, and may God bless you all one hundred fold"?

Scriptures Chapter 13

1. **1 Timothy 6:10** For the love of money is the root of all evil . . .
2. **Matthew 13:12** For whosoever hath, to him shall be given, and he shall have more abundance . . .
3. **John 10:10** I am come that they might have life, and that they might have *it* more abundantly.
4. **3 John 1:2** Beloved, I wish above all things that thou mayest prosper and be in health, even as thy soul prospereth.
5. **Philippians 4:19** But my God shall supply all your need according to his riches in glory by Christ Jesus.
6. **Psalm 50:10** For every beast of the forest *is* mine, *and* the cattle upon a thousand hills.
7. **Psalms 50:14** Offer unto God thanksgiving; and pay thy vows unto the most High . . .
8. **Psalms 50:15** And call upon me in the day of trouble: I will deliver thee, and thou shalt glorify me.
9. **James 1:8** A double-minded man *is* unstable in all his ways.
10. **Matthew 18:19** . . .That if two of you shall agree on earth as touching any thing that they shall ask, it shall be done for them of my Father which is in Heaven.
11. **Matt 18:20** For where two or three are gathered together in my name, there am I in the midst of them.

12. **Deuteronomy 14:22, Nehemiah 10:37, Matthew 23:23, Luke 11:42, Luke 18:12, Hebrews:5**

13. **Genesis 14:20, Leviticus 27:30, Numbers 18:24, Deuteronomy 12:6, Deuteronomy 14:23, 2 Deuteronomy 26:12**

14. **2 Chronicles 31:5, Nehemiah 12:44, Nehemiah 13:5, Amos 4:4, Malachi 3:10**

15. **Hebrew 7:9** . . . Levi also, who receiveth tithes, payed tithes in . . .

16. **Acts 3:6** . . . Silver and gold have I none; but such as I have give I thee: In the name of Jesus Christ of Nazareth, rise up and walk.

Chapter 14
*Blessed Are They That Hunger and Thirst
For They Shall Be Filled*

Many people want to hear the word. We go to church, listen to sermons, and Christian books continue to be written. Those of us doing these things must want to know God and his word or we wouldn't be doing them. But how many have considered and know what it means to hunger and thirst after righteousness? To me, it means to need or want more than you are getting. Have you ever been really hungry? Stop all your other thoughts for a moment and picture this in your mind. What does hunger feel like? Can you feel it? Now picture God and his word as your favorite food. It's the best thing in the world for you, and you can have as much or as little as you want. The more you eat of this food the stronger, healthier and wiser you become. This same food can make every aspect of your life perfect, from your body to your husband, children, home and job. Now decide every day how hungry you are and how much you want. The greatest teachings in the world cannot make you stay hungry for spirit food by teaching you God's word on Saturdays or Sundays for an hour. The teaching may be encouraging or touching, but when you leave there those feelings will only last so long when your life of reality hits you, and you don't know how to find God's direction. So here's what to do. You have to make a conscious choice to seek God and search for his answers and direction every day. The more you do this, the easier it is, because this is what lets God know that your free-will desire is for him to direct you. In reality, our traditional church gatherings are causing many of our teachers to be holding people back in spite of their desire to bring them closer to God. The setup of the traditional church causes an inability to teach people on the individual levels of each person present. Also, time does not allow them to teach how to receive the things they preached on being available. It's time to make changes in our acceptance of this to ensure that none are being left out, or more importantly, left behind. You have to want and be hungry for more than this or things will never change. God and his word will always be a mystery to people if they can't make it their own.[1]

The only way to truly know the spiritual depth of God is to have a hunger and thirst and to have a true from-your-heart desire. This is what God meant in this clue he gave us: "Thy word have I hid in my heart that I might not sin against thee."[2] God's word also says, "And ye shall seek me, and find me when you search for me with your whole heart."[3] For he said, if you "hunger and thirst after righteousness, you shall be filled."[4]

Have you ever not realized how hungry you were until you started eating or thinking about food? When you are hungry, do you wait until Sunday to eat? In order to understand spiritual things, we have to have a desire and a spiritual hunger, be looking at things through spiritual eyes and listening with spiritual ears, with a hunger, thirst and desire to know God every day. You have to know him to love him. How can we love someone we do not truly know? Where is the heart's desire if we don't want to hear or talk about the Bible until Sunday? This is one thing I do know for myself: I want God's presence in my life every second of every day because he is so wonderful.

God's word says that those who hunger and thirst after righteousness shall be filled. Notice he said shall be, not might be. He also said that the natural man receives not the things of the spirit of God, for they are foolishness unto him, neither can he know them for they are spiritually discerned. You cannot see spiritual things through natural eyes. If you have been limited from knowing Jesus and who he is, you remain a natural man.

Many of our ministers, pastors and teachers are teaching us the word by trying to find different ways to say what God said so we can understand it easier. But when God's word is changed, how will you know you are following God if you don't go home and study what they taught, and make sure it's God's truth and not that teacher's? This is why you are to be doers of the word and not hearers only. If you do not study and search what a man or minister has said, you are only a hearer, deceiving yourself thinking you know the truth from

God. The word says, "These were more noble than those, for they searched the scriptures daily whether these things were so."

If all we remember are some of the verses and scriptures, and we don't understand the gift that is in us through knowing Jesus Christ, God cannot give the increase. So we end up still confused and having to rely on the teacher for spiritual growth. If you do not have a personal relationship of love, communication and understanding with God, and if it is not full of excitement, then you should ask yourself, is it possible that someone has limited you with wrong teaching? Even if it is one thing they are wrong about, they have limited you in that area.

God's word in Ephesians 4:13 says, "Till we all come in the unity of faith [we all agree], and of the knowledge of the Son of God, unto a perfect man . . ."[5] Ephesians 4:14 says, "That we henceforth [from then on] be no more children, tossed to and fro and carried about with every wind of doctrine."[6, 7] This means everyone who comes along has a great speech or a good doctrine. They know what we should do with our lives, and they tell us what God's word says we should do. We follow what sounds best at the time until something that sounds better, or easier, comes up (tossed to and fro). We will continue to be tossed if we cannot read it ourselves and understand it, because we are at their mercy instead of God's.

I have spoken the word to so many people, and what I find most is that many of them have little or no understanding of the whole plan and purpose written in the Bible. His word says that if a person has a form of godliness, but they deny the power therein, "from such turn away."[8] If our teachers are not teaching us about the power we have through Christ, God's word says turn away. If you have been taught God's truth, and have believed in God and his word for years, then by now you should be confidently doing the same things Christ did.

God's children should be full of excitement because of the signs, miracles, wonders and angels in their lives. If you are being taught the truth from God's word, that same word says these things are available. You should be living these promises and not still just be looking for them and talking about them. Each and every one of God's children has been given by God the ability to walk with signs, miracles and wonders. You should be learning how to receive these from God, no matter what church you go to. This is God's truth. So I ask you, do you have these things? Or are you getting hungry?

If you ask a person if they go to church, or ask them what church they go to, most will hesitantly tell you. Then, when you try to carry on a conversation with them about it, mentioning God or Satan, most of them, like in politics, will discreetly change the subject. I believe one of the biggest reasons for this is because we have so many different beliefs, and so much lack of understanding, that people are not comfortable or confident talking about it.

Have you ever tried to talk to people on a Tuesday about God, his word or Satan? How long will they chat before changing the subject or running? The sad part is that many are still running from things when they get to church on Sunday. They sit there in church, trying to figure out why the children in this world are turning out the way they are. Why do we allow the garbage from the television and internet, why are so many not prosperous, why is the world such a mess and how can we possibly fix it, when God has already given us all of these answers? Many good people just haven't been taught the truth. Are we hearers of the word or are we doers? And which one do we want to be?

Those who truly want to know God and live by his word need to be doers. Learn it, understand it, speak it and live it. Your life is not going to change and you will not receive all the promises of God just because you hear it and it sounds good. It is up to you to make it your own and apply it. It's time to bring God's people together; it is available. The word says that with God, all things are possible through Christ.

It's no wonder the world is such a mess. People are not likeminded about anything, and everyone thinks they are right. What is there to document they're not right if there is no common ground? What are the rules if we can all use a different book? God says search his scriptures, not the minds and books of the world, whether these things are so.

This is the design of God's word. It is the rulebook for life and living, but we who love God have turned it into a religious social event with rules that go against the word of God. What would happen if everyone who truly loves God followed the same book and made a stand? No more making our own laws and rules. And what if we simply followed God's laws and rules and asked Jesus, "Master, what is the greatest commandment?" I'm sure he would still say, "Love God first with all your heart, soul, mind and strength. Love your neighbor as yourselves and on these two commandments hang all the laws and all the prophets."

Are we seeking first the kingdom of God and his righteousness, or is it possible we are following prophets and teachers not knowing whether they are false or not because we don't know what else to do? God is your personal Father and his word is your personal love letter. Can the people who love God come together in the unity of Christ and make a stand to claim it for our own and know for sure we have his truth? His word says:

> Mark 10:27 . . . with God, all things are possible.
>
> Luke 18:27 . . . The things which are impossible with men, are possible with God.
>
> Matthew 19:26 . . . but with God all things are possible.
>
> Mark 9:23 . . . all things are possible to him that believeth.

Scriptures, Chapter 14

Read the following messages to you from God

1. **Matthew 6:33** But seek ye first the kingdom of God, and his righteousness; and all these things shall be added unto you.
2. **Psalms 119:11** Thy word have I hid in mine heart, that I might not sin against thee.
3. **Jeremiah 29:13** And ye shall seek me, and find me, when ye shall search for me with all your heart.
4. **Matthew 5:6** Blessed are they which do hunger and thirst after righteousness: for they shall be filled.
5. **Ephesians 4:13** Till we all come in the unity of faith, and of the knowledge of the Son of God, unto a perfect man . . .

6. **Ephesians 4:14** That we henceforth be no more children, tossed to and fro and carried about with every wind of doctrine . . .

7. **2 Peter 2:1** But there were false prophets also among the people, even as there shall be false teachers among you, who privily shall bring in damnable heresies, even denying the Lord that bought them, and bring upon them selves swift destruction.

8. **2 Timothy 3:5** . . . Having a form of godliness, but denying the power thereof: from such turn away.

Chapter 15
Denominational Differences

I write this with great heart for God's truth to be revealed so that his children may come together. I have no desire to criticize but to bring together information to study for documentation of facts. So I will start with the background and story of this chapter, the same way I have shared my other experiences since I was introduced to our Father.

The day I started writing this book I was told, just write, and that it would come together in the end, so I started writing. The next chapter you will be reading, "Is Jesus Christ God," was the first chapter I put on paper. How it ended up, behind what I tell you today, and why I write this final chapter before you read it, may seem a little strange in a book, but this is briefly how it came together.

Four months in, I had quite a bit written in this book, but it had no form or corrections. I struggled with slight embarrassment at that time, wondering how many people might not be able to see it as God's simple truth and would think what I was writing was foolishness. I did not understand why I was inspired to start having others read it, when at that point it still needed so much work. I swallowed my pride and followed God's direction. As it turned out, the book was being edited as it was still in the writing process, which is now obvious that it was part of God's plan to get it to you faster and better through the input of others. Every person who read it gave insight from different levels of understanding in the word and they were all very encouraging.

One day as I was writing, I prayed and asked God, how can I be sure that I am teaching your truth on this subject, if I have not thoroughly studied and searched what other denominations are teaching? The next thing I knew I had the phone book out and was calling a church of a different denomination to talk to a minister. Since that day, I have had conversations with six other people from different denominations, and each one of them was very open for discussion of our faith. I had several questions they could not answer, so they provided me with the information people use to document the belief that Jesus Christ is God. I have studied them as well as the statements of faith that I received. I have read, studied and searched the information with an open mind, truly wanting to know. I continually prayed and considered my own cautions for accurately teaching the truth of God's word so as not to be a false teacher myself, and because this is a critical subject that we disagree on in our Christian stand. I have to say in all my praying, studying and searching, I am more convinced than ever that many people need to re-study this subject for themselves in prayer because according to God, our eternal life depends on this one answer.

The following information is documented and available to the public, so I would like to share with you my reasons for making the previous bold statement. This is why I believe Jesus Christ is the Son of God. I will share just a few of the things I found in the writings and documentations I received, as I tried to line them up with the scriptures from God in the Bible. Again, I encourage people to read these things for comprehension and understanding, and follow in your Bible as these things are taught. Read the context around what is being said, and make sure you understand it. One of God's promises to you is that he is not the author of confusion. If something does not fit, stop and find out why. This is your eternal life that is on the line.

One of the forms I was given said this in the opening statement: "Jesus claimed to be God." Just because these documents and forms say he did, does not make that true. I want someone to show us in what chapter and verse Jesus said, I am God your Father, or anything similar. There is only one scripture I can find that is not crystal clear on the surface and they use it to tell us Jesus said he is also God. This verse is John 10:30. He said, "I and my Father are one." If I said, "I and my son are one," would you think we were one person? No, that is not possible. We can be likeminded or of the same bodily form or nature, but my son and I are still two beings. In the chapter following this, I have shown using the context of those scriptures why Jesus made that statement. So, for now, let us ask ourselves some questions.

How many times did Jesus tell us he was not God?

How many times did he say he is the Son of God?

How many times did God or Jesus refer to God's love for his Son?

The answer to each of these questions is many times. Several of them are listed for you in chapter 16 with scripture reference. God or his word did not lie in any of those statements, so why did he say them?

Read John 8:16–18, and ask yourself why Jesus himself said, "And yet if I judge, my judgment is true: for I am not alone, but I and the Father that sent me. It is also written in your law, that the testimony of two men is true. I am one that bear witness of myself, and the Father that sent me beareth witness of me." Jesus just said himself that they are two witnesses.

This is another verse that is being used to indicate that Jesus is God: John 14:9, "He that hath seen me hath seen the Father." I encourage you to read John 14:6-12 and keep in mind while you read this that John 1:18 says, "No man hath seen God at any time." Many people saw Jesus; he was being seen by people even in scriptures they are using to say he was God. 1 John 4:12 says this same thing, "No man hath seen God at any time." John 4:13 says, "And we have seen and do testify that the Father sent the Son to be the Saviour of the world. Whosoever shall confess that Jesus is the Son of God, God dwelleth in him, and he in God." This is what the Bible says, and this is what I choose to believe.

Jesus also said to doubting Thomas, "Because you have seen me, you have believed." So if Jesus said people had seen him, to think he was God would make God a liar. Also understand what it says in Romans 10:9-10, "If you shall confess with your mouth the Lord Jesus, and shall believe in your heart that God has raised him from the dead you shall be saved."

Another common scripture they have used is John 1:1-3. Notice we are in the same chapter where we just read no man hath ever seen God at any time. "In the beginning was the word and the word was with God and the word was God. The same was in the beginning with God." Verse 3 says, "All things were made by him; and without him was not any thing made that was made." What we just read does not tell us that Jesus was with God before he was born but that is the teaching of this. The word being made flesh was not even told until verse 14; this flesh was Jesus. Before this it says God was the light of the world, and the world knew him not; that is why he sent his Son in the flesh to declare him in verse 18. Read in your Bible at least through verse 34. Verse 14 says, "the word was made flesh and dwelt among us." Two verses after that in 18, it says, "No man has seen the father at any time." I ask you, which of the following statements are confusing and could be lies according to the Bible?

People have seen God in the flesh and spent time with him.

In the beginning Jesus was with God and he was God before he was born.

We have two Gods. One is a spirit and the other was a God of flesh who goes by the name of Jesus. He was walking the earth, praying and talking to himself, saying things to confuse us.

All of these are lies according to God and his word.

I am sorry, but I cannot be convinced. I still choose to believe what God said for me to believe, "Whosoever shall confess that Jesus is the Son of God, God dwelleth in him, and he in God."

What concerns me the most is that no person, preacher, teacher or individual could explain this without going outside of the Bible to information they have been given which cannot even be documented by God's word, and that's what they say they are teaching us (God's word). And even then, it doesn't make sense if you listen and think about what they are saying. I always get the same answers when I ask why this is. They will say, "Many things you just have to take in faith, or, "many things in the word are a mystery." Well, that same word they say has mysteries tells us God reveals all mysteries to those who know him. Yes, we are to have faith, but it never says follow faith blindly. According to God, Satan is the only one who blinds anything.

I realize I am making a bold stand. Yes, I have been accused of and have heard the word cult, but I am not telling you to follow me. You should follow God's word if that is what you are following. I am confident telling you that I am standing on God's words. Did God so love the world that he gave his only begotten self? No, that is not what he said; he said, "his only begotten Son. That whosoever shall believe in his Son shall not perish but have everlasting life." How can we believe in something we cannot explain and have it make sense? As you read the next chapter, you will see God's word is not the mystery it's made out to be. This is done by using documented scriptures.

God said search his scriptures; he did not say search the doctrines of men.

It was a little less than eight months ago that I had the debate with God about writing this book, and there is no question it has come to you so quickly through Christ which strengthened me and my family and loved ones. I could write another book just about the signs, miracles and wonders through its progress. But that is not meant to be. So all I will say is this: be cautious. Think about what you are accepting as truth. Satan can imitate the light.

Not wanting to leave any room for error, I have tried to do a study on the word trinity or triune God. I have confirmed that God, in his word, never used those words in regard to himself or to Jesus or in reference to the Spirit. Having no scriptures to use for documentation of facts from God on this subject and because of God's many warnings such as, "beware of false teachers." I felt a need to look at this closer, in order to make sure I have considered all the facts that others use to document that Jesus was God.

I spent three hours with a wonderful man. He agreed with me that we truly want to know who is right according to God and not man because our eternal life is dependent on this one answer. So by questioning and studying their understanding of God's word, this is what I found: The churches that teach this say that the trinity means the Father and the Son and the Holy Ghost are all one and the same. They are God and that God walked this earth as a man. They also say that Jesus was God in the flesh, but that he is also God's Son. Some of the first questions I had for this man were, "How can we be reading the same book and have different truths? Because there can only be one truth! And how do we know who is right?"

He said, "I have had those same questions myself." Well my answer to him was, "Only God can be right!" So I asked him to explain and show me how and where they get the information to document this understanding from the word.

The first thing he said was that "we believe, Jesus made the church the custodians of the word, and the word does not always mean the Bible." He also said that there was a man named Ignatius who wrote a book to the Ephesians in early Christian writings and that they follow his doctrine. He gave me a copy of these writings and I studied them and searched the word and could not find anything to document these early Christian writings, so, this tells me they have gone outside of God's word for these teachings. Anything outside of God's word is not God's word. You cannot learn social studies out of a math book.

Remember God's scriptures, that which we already know he has said on this subject. "Search the scriptures," and, "Thy word have I hid in mine heart," also, "Search the scriptures daily whether these things are so." These are just a few that direct us to stay in his word and his scriptures.

Here is my new question that came up as I studied this. If this teaching is correct according to God's word, why did God not mention any of these words or names in the Bible? I looked for them, and the Bible never mentioned Ignatius or custodians in his word or early Christian writings in the Bible. So how do we know that this man Ignatius is of God? Where is he documented from God to have credibility? This wonderful man that I met with also said that they believe this man, Ignatius, was there with the apostles, and that he also witnessed things that were not written in the Bible.

This part I knew was true. It does say in the word that things were said and done that were not written in the Bible because the book could not contain it all. But if this man had critical information for us, I do not believe God would have left him or his name out of his word, which is our only documentation for hope. This study material is public information. Read and study it with your King James Bible and confirm it before you follow or believe anything.

New rewritten books and Bibles may be easier to read but what good does it do to understand it if it's untrue and changes what God originally said? If you wanted to be a lawyer, no one is going to rewrite the law books to make it easier for you. You have to learn it and say it the way it is written. And you cannot become a doctor by learning that the leg is connected to the foot. Your desire and choices will ensure that you learn and understand whatever you study with desire, even the Bible.

There can only be one truth, and how do we know who is right? ONLY GOD IS; anything else is not God's true word!

If you are following a dream, and the words that describe that dream are not in God's word, then you're chasing a dream you will never find. Because God said there is nothing new under the sun.

I will always remember what a great man of God once said, and he changed my life forever, "That the word of God fits together like a hand fits in a glove, and it works with a mathematical exactness and a scientific precision." Wow, what a true statement.

> 1 John 5:13: "These things have I written unto you that believe on the name of the Son of God; that ye may know that ye have eternal life, and that ye may believe on the name of the Son of God."

Chapter 16
Rightly Dividing the Word: Is Jesus Christ God?

Let's settle the question that, according to God himself, is the most important question in the world today. After studying God's word, you decide. Who is Jesus Christ? Is he God? Remember 1 John 4:12 "No man hath seen God at any time . . ." There can only be one truth. How do we know for sure who is right? This is what God's word says in James 1:22, "But be ye doers of the word, and not hearers only, deceiving your own selves." Jesus Christ says in John 5:39, "Search the scriptures; for in them ye think ye have eternal life: and they are they which testify of me." Read these words carefully. Jesus Christ said this for a reason, so take note. Learn to read God's word and do not read into it or over it.

Jesus Christ also said in John 14:6 that "No man can come unto the Father but by me." After reading these verses, I think we should all want to know for sure who Jesus Christ is according to God and not the world. So let's "study to show ourselves approved unto God as a workman and rightly divide the word of truth" to find the answer to this question. To rightly divide the word also means we can wrongly divide it, or God would have simply said, "Divide it."

God is not the author of confusion, and he advises us to be wise as serpents. We need to use the common sense that he gave us so we are not tossed to and fro or misled by false teachers. God's word is perfect and we must be sure we read and understand every word. Even the smallest word can change or enhance the meaning of what he actually said. Here is one example of small words with big importance. Ephesians 1:17, "That the God of our Lord Jesus Christ, the Father of glory, may give unto you the spirit of wisdom and revelation in the knowledge of him." Notice the importance of the smaller words, "The God of our Lord Jesus Christ, the Father of glory." The words *the* and *of* indicates that they are two separate individuals. Now test the facts, and reread this same verse without *the* and *of*. "That God our Lord Jesus Christ, Father of Glory." Now this says that God and Jesus are the same. Just by taking out two small words, "the" and "of," we have changed God's word to say the exact opposite of who God actually said they are.

I make this point to show how important it is to read and understand even the small words. This is what it takes to be a workman of the word, studying to rightly divide and to search the scriptures for God's truth. God would not mince words. He is God. He is perfect and so is his word. Just read it.

Before we start this study of the scriptures, we should take a moment to thank God for clearing our minds from the world's teachings. Don't take anyone's word for truth as if it's from God. Study it, and know what God said.

The best way to know for sure what God says about any subject is to take each scripture God used that pertains to the subject in question and read it very carefully. Know what he has said, make sure you understand it and then make sure it does not contradict any of the other things God said throughout his word. If it does contradict something, then study to find out why. It could be in your understanding because of things you have heard or have been taught, or there could be an error in the translation. Ask yourself what the verse says. Make sure you know the context surrounding it and the message.

We have been listening to the world for so long that God's easy-to-find answers are hard to accept and hold on to. The object of this is to assist people in rightly dividing and understanding God's word and to find his truths. According to God's word, there are many people who only think they have eternal life, but they don't if they don't know for sure who Jesus Christ really is. I have used the following pattern to be sure I understand what God said. Read each of the following scriptures carefully; do not read over them or into them. Answer the following scriptures. What are the scriptures saying? If you would like, put a check mark next to the answers to establish for yourself what God said. Does the Bible say they are Father and Son or are they one in the same? If you truly want God's truth you must not hold on to what you have been taught. The following scriptures are God's words, not mine or your teachers'. Stay wise and read what God said in each verse.

John 3:16 "For God so loved the world, that he gave his only begotten Son, that whosoever believeth in him should not perish, but have everlasting life."

Father and Son separate beings____ one and the same____

John 3:18 "He that believeth in him is not condemned: but he that believeth not is condemned already, because he hath not believed in the name of the only begotten Son of God."

Father and Son separate beings____ one and the same____

John 3:34 "For he whom God hath sent speaketh the words of God: for God giveth not the Spirit by measure."

Father and Son separate beings____ one and the same____

John 3:35 "The Father loveth the Son, and hath given all things into his hand."

Father and Son separate beings____ one and the same____

John 3:36 "He that believeth on the Son hath everlasting life: and he that believeth not on the Son shall not see life; but the wrath of God abideth on him."

Father and Son separate beings____ one and the same____

John 8:16 "And yet if I judge, my judgment is true: for I am not alone, but I and the Father that sent me."

Father and Son separate beings____ one and the same____

John 8:26 "I have many things to say and to judge of you: but he that sent me is true; and I speak to the world those things which I have heard of him."

Father and Son separate beings____ one and the same____

John 8:42 . . . I proceedeth forth and came from God: neither came I of myself, but he sent me.

Father and Son separate beings____ one and the same____

John 14:10 . . . the words that I speak unto you I speak not of myself: but the Father that dwelleth in me, he doeth the works.

Father and Son separate beings____ one and the same____

John 6:44 No man can come to me, except the Father which hath sent me draw him . . .

Father and Son separate beings____ one and the same____

John 12:44 . . . believe not on me, but on him that sent me.

Father and Son separate beings____ one and the same____

John 12:49 "For I have not spoken of myself; but the Father which sent me, he gave me a commandment, what I should say, and what I should speak."

Father and Son separate beings____ one and the same____

John 14:1 "Let not your heart be troubled: ye believe in God, believe also in me."

Father and Son separate beings____ one and the same____

John 14:2 "In my Father's house are many mansions: if it were not so, I would have told you I go to prepare a place for you."

Father and Son separate beings____ one and the same____

John 14:12 "Verily, verily, I say unto you, He that believeth on me, the works that I do shall he do also; and greater works than these shall he do; because I go unto my Father."

Father and Son separate beings____ one and the same____

Acts 3:26 "Unto you first God, having raised up his Son Jesus, sent him to bless you. . ."

Father and Son separate beings____ one and the same____

Romans 10: 9 "That if thou shalt confess with thy mouth the Lord Jesus and shalt believe in thine heart that God hath raised him from the dead thou shalt be saved."

Father and Son separate beings____ one and the same____

Galatians 1:1 "Paul, an apostle, (not of men, neither by men, but by Jesus Christ, and God the Father, who raised him from the dead;")

Father and Son separate beings____ one and the same____

Ephesians 1:20 "Which he wrought in Christ, when he raised him from the dead, and set him at his own right hand in the heavenly places."

Father and Son separate beings____ one and the same____

Ephesians 1:17 "That the God of our Lord Jesus Christ, the Father of glory, may give unto you the spirit of wisdom and revelation in the knowledge of him."

Father and Son separate beings____ one and the same____

Ephesians 4:13 "Till we all come in the unity of the faith, and of the knowledge of the Son of God, unto a perfect man . . ." [Unity of faith means until we all agree.]

Father and Son separate beings____ one and the same____

1 Timothy 2:5 "For there is one God, and one mediator between God and men the man Christ Jesus."

Father and Son separate beings____ one and the same____

1 John 1:3 ". . . and truly our fellowship is with the Father and with the Son Jesus Christ."

Father and Son separate beings____ one and the same____

1 John 1:7 ". . . and the blood of Jesus Christ his Son cleanseth us from all sin."

Father and Son separate beings____ one and the same____

1 John 2:23 "Whosoever denieth the Son, the same hath not the Father . . ."

Father and Son separate beings____ one and the same____

1 John 5:5 "Who is he that overcometh the world, but he that believeth that Jesus is the Son of God?"

Father and Son separate beings____ one and the same____

Matthew 27:43 ". . .for he said, I am the Son of God."

Father and Son separate beings____ one and the same____

Matthew 26:39 ". . . O my Father if it be possible, let this cup pass from me, nevertheless not as I will but as thou wilt."

Father and Son separate beings____ one and the same____

John 13:3 Jesus knowing that the Father had given all things into his hands, and that he was come from God and went to God.

Father and Son separate beings____ one and the same____

Now let's look at some of the verses that are not so straight to the point and find out why there are apparent contradictions, because God is not the author of confusion and he did not lie.

Ephesians 4:5 "One Lord, one faith, one baptism."

Father and Son separate beings____ one and the same____

Ephesians 4:6 "One God and Father of all, who is above all and through all and in you all."

Father and Son separate beings____ one and the same____

Notice how short verse 5 is, then note the next verse and consider the punctuation we saw earlier in the study and read them together as one verse, and you decide. Could this be man's error that caused this to contradict so many other scriptures?

Ephesians 4:5–6 "One Lord, one faith, one baptism. One God and Father of all, who is above all, through all and in you all."

Father and Son separate beings____ one and the same____

Now then we come to John 10:30 "I and my Father are one"

Father and Son separate beings____ one and the same____

Note the context (all of what was being said) in the verses before and after this one.

John 10:29 "My Father which gave them me is greater than all;"

Father and Son separate beings____ one and the same____

John 10:32 "Jesus answered them, Many good works have I shewed you from my Father; for which of those works do ye stone me."

Father and Son separate beings____ one and the same____

John 4:24 "God is a spirit." (Notice this was said in the book of John while Jesus Christ was walking the earth as a man.)

Num 23:19 "God is not a man, that he should lie . . ."

We have already read 1 Tim 2:5 that referred to the man Christ Jesus.

John 8:58 "Jesus said unto them, . . . I say unto you, before Abraham was, I am."

Jesus Christ said many times, I am. He said I am the door, I am the light and he also said I am the Lamb, to name a few. But he never said I am the Father, or I am he who sent me. Jesus Christ never minced his words.

God says to be wise as serpents and meek as doves, so he expects us to use our wisdom and logic. I want you to really read the following scriptures. As he warns us in 2 Peter 2:1, ". . . there shall be false teachers among you, who privily shall bring in damnable heresies, even denying the Lord that brought them." 2 Peter 2:2 says, "And bring upon themselves swift destruction and many will follow their pernicious ways, by reason of whom the way of truth shall be evil spoken of." He also says to his disciples in Luke 20:46, "Beware of the scribes, which desire to walk in long robes, and love greetings in the markets, and the highest seats in the synagogues, and the chief rooms at feasts."

So no matter who has taught us, let's rightly divide the word using logic and wisdom to find out from God if we have been wrongly taught from our teachers.

Here are a few questions for us to ask ourselves and the teachers who teach that Jesus Christ is God. Show us the answers to these questions from the Bible alone. God said be wise as serpents.

I have counted eighty-seven verses in God's word (the Bible) that specifically say he is the Son of God. How many specifically say he is God?

Why can't I find at least one verse that specifically says Jesus is God, when they were both so adamant to say he was not?
Why would God intentionally confuse us so many times?

If Jesus Christ was God, why would he have asked himself if this cup could be passed from him? If he were God, wouldn't he have known the plan?

Who was Jesus Christ talking about when he said, let your will be done not mine?

If Jesus was God, why did he say, "Forgive them Father for they know not what they do"? If he was God, wouldn't he have said, "I forgive you, for you know not what you do"?

If a man is dead for three days and three nights, can he do anything? No, not even God could raise himself if he was really dead.

Did God go unto himself to be seated at his own right hand? Have you ever tried to sit at your own right hand?

If God and Jesus are the same, why did God pray to himself?

Why did Jesus say so many times, things like, I do the will of my Father?

Why is Jesus Christ the one coming to gather us? Why not God himself?

Do we now have two Gods in heaven since we have to go through Jesus?

Why did God say, this is my beloved Son in whom I am well pleased? Was he patting himself on the back because he was so pleased with himself?

If Jesus was God, why did Jesus inform us that God entrusted him with judgment?

Why does he still go by Jesus if they were both God?

If Jesus is God why do we need to call him Lord or Jesus and then call him God in the same sentence?

How do we know when to use the different names?

We hear teachings all the time talking about Jesus, and they say things like, "Jesus knows these things because he is God," and in the same sermon a short time later say, "God had his wrath upon Jesus." If Jesus was God, why do you not call him God throughout the teaching? Also wouldn't that wrath have been on God himself?

These types of sermons sound pretty confusing to me. And God told us there is confusion in every evil work. God was warning us when he said that he is not the author of confusion. God would not have put all these verses in his word to confuse us, and then tell us in the same book that there is confusion in every evil work.

God said we should be wise as serpents, so why do these teachings not line up when we look closely at other facts like when Jesus was on the cross and what God's word says happened? In Matthew 27:43 it says, "Jesus trusted in God, for he said; I am the Son of God." In Matthew 27:54, "When the earth quaked, the people said, truly this was the Son of God," which tells us they finally, at that moment, believed what Jesus had been trying to tell them, that he was God's Son. This is documented in John 10:30 Jesus said, "I and my father are one." He said this because they were likeminded, meaning the same mission and goal, which is proven in the context of the scriptures before and after he made that statement.

Let's read and find out what happened according to the scriptures. The context of John chapter 10 explains why Jesus said this in verse 30 ("I and my Father are one"). Also notice he said, "I and my Father" (two beings). To fully understand it, we need to start in John 9:7, "Jesus healed the man that was blind from birth," and 9:15, "So the Jews brought this man to the Pharisees and they were judging Jesus, and accusing him for healing the man on the Sabbath day." And 9:35, "Jesus asked the blind man, 'dost thou believe on the Son of God?' The blind man said, 'Who is he that I might believe on him?'" And 9:37, "And Jesus said, 'Thou hast seen him and it is he [the Son] that talks with thee.' The Pharisees heard this and asked, 'Are we blind also?'" So Jesus was talking to them (the Pharisees), when he said, in John 10:9, "I am the door: by me if any man enter in he shall be saved." Then he said, "the thief cometh not but to steal and to kill and to destroy: I am come that they might have life, and that they might have it more abundantly."

In verse 15 he documents again who he is when he said, "As the Father knows me, even so know I the Father," and verse 17, "Therefore doth my Father love me." He wasn't saying he loved himself. And again in verse 18, "This commandment have I received of my Father." In 10:24, "The Jews said, 'If thou be the Christ, tell us plainly.' Jesus said, 'I told you, and you believed not.'" Jesus in

10:29 again establishes that he is the Son of God when he said, "My Father which gave me is greater than all, and no man is able to pluck out of my Father's hand." After all this, in verse 30, why did Jesus say, "I and my Father are one"? Notice he still referred to God as his Father, but the biggest key here is what was going on. Jesus was telling them it is not unlawful to claim to be gods, but you are accusing me because I said I am the Son of God. Verse 36 says, "Say ye of him, whom the Father hath sanctified, and sent into the world, thou blasphemest [speak injuriously]; because I said, 'I am the Son of God.'" So when Jesus said, "I and my Father are one." He said, "I and my Father," which could not mean one being. He was saying they were likeminded, because he already told us no man can come unto the Father if we don't know him (the Son of God).

Consider this also: God's word says that two shall become one in a marriage between a husband and wife. Genesis 2:24 says, ". . . and shall cleave unto his wife: and they shall be one flesh." We say that I and my husband are one. Do we become the same person? No, he meant we are likeminded, always thinking the same, always knowing each other's thoughts and with the same goals in mind. This is how Jesus and the Father were one.

We must take great caution when someone tells us what the Bible says. If we neglect to consider one word or verse from God's word without great caution, we could be in trouble. I know of two verses of scripture, Psalms 14:1 and Psalms 53:1, a person could show you that says, "there is no God"; if you let them leave out the words before it that says, "the fool hath said in his heart that there is no God."

Faith coupled with wisdom = CONFIDENCE.

Chapter 17
The Plan and Purpose of Christ and Him Crucified

We know from the study of John 1:1 that God's word was with him in the beginning before he created the heavens and the earth, so he obviously had a plan. The plan and purpose of Christ is revealed throughout his word. If we do not understand this plan, we cannot fully see the glory of his victory or claim the benefits from all that he achieved. Every one of these details is laid out for us in the pages of scriptures. In order to find them we must search the scriptures and study. This means to compile or document all the facts from God's word, and continuing to bring every new thought to what we already know was said: this is how to confirm it as God's truth. Let's start in the beginning like God did and gather the facts. What happened in the Garden of Eden? (Remember, we will be gathering facts for the next few verses.)

We know Adam and Eve sinned and died a spiritual death; they lost the spiritual connection with God. Also remember God had given Adam dominion, or ownership, of the world. When they sinned, they gave the ownership to Satan. To document this, God's word referred to Satan as the god of this world. Another point to this was when Satan tempted Jesus in the wilderness. Satan pointed to the world and said, "All these things I give thee, if thou wilt fall down and worship me." Satan and Jesus both knew Satan owned it, because he could not have given something he did not own. Jesus did not deny it. Jesus would have simply said I already own it.

Jesus Christ was the purchase price God paid to buy us back from Satan. This purchase with his blood is documented in 1 Corinthians 6:20, "For ye are bought with a price." In 1 Corinthians 7:23, "ye are bought with a price." Also Acts 20:28, ". . . which he hath purchased with his own blood." What was bought was the spirit Adam and Eve lost. The purchase price for this was the blood of Christ. God did not die for us; his Son did—his only begotten Son—which means his biological son, the seed he planted in Mary.

These are some thoughts we should consider: What was the price that was paid? If God was Jesus and he died—knowing it was only for three days and three nights—and he would still be alive enough to know when seventy-two hours were up and raise himself? No, the purchase price was that his only begotten Son had to die in order to save us.

Consider Jesus Christ saying to God, "If this cup can be passed from me." Jesus Christ did not want to die, because he did not know yet the full plan and purpose his Father had for his death. This is why Jesus said, "Let thy will be done and not mine." He did not know his Father's plan and God could not have revealed it until the last second. This is documented in 1 Corinthians 2:8 where it says, ". . . which none of the princes of this world knew: for had they known, they would not have crucified the Lord of glory."

Now then, what happened on the cross? In Matthew 27:46, the translators added, "this is to say." And in Mark 15:34 they added the words, ". . .which is being interpreted to say. . ." Why twice then, when translating this, did they say what Jesus said was being interpreted? And why, in these two scriptures, did they choose to leave in the original language, E'-li, E'-li, la'ma sabach'tha-ni? And then say, "which is being interpreted, 'My God my God why hast thou forsaken me.'" Interpreted by whom? Read 2 Peter 1:20, "Knowing this first, that no prophecy of the scripture is of any private interpretation." Are we accepting that God forsook his Son in whom he was well pleased? These types of things should be a red flag for us to stop and do what God told us to do. Bring it captive with the rest of the word. Search, study and meditate on it, asking ourselves, "Dost thou understandest what thou readest?" What else is this saying. To those who say this was God on the cross it says that God forsook himself, and then asked himself why he was doing it. Remember, some say this was God on the cross when you read it again, "My God my God why hast thou forsaken me." It also contradicts Luke 23:46, "Jesus said; 'Father, into thy hands I commend my spirit,' and he gave up the ghost." Bringing all facts together that we have gathered from the word is what establishes the masterpiece of God's matchless word, and how it fits together with perfection from cover to cover.

Jesus did not know the plan until God revealed it to him when he was on the cross. Remember, Jesus had asked God if this cup could be passed from him. He said, "Let thy will be done and not mine." He knew he had to die, but he still did not know the bigger plan. His death would give us back the spirit that Adam and Eve sinned away and even better than that which they had, because they could lose the spirit; we cannot. The spirit is in us and cannot be sinned away. This is what is called, "Christ in you," the hope of glory. The reason God also referred to this as being born again was because one that is born cannot become unborn. If you study this, you will find that at that moment, when Jesus was on the cross, God revealed his plan to him. And Jesus gave up the ghost saying, in Estrangelo Aramaic (correct translation), "My God my God for this purpose was I spared, for this purpose was I kept." This cry of victory would document God's love, not a cry of defeat. This is also confirmed by all the other facts in the word. God not forsaking himself is only one of the many confusing contradictions that no longer exist. What if this is the correct translation from the Estrangelo Aramaic to the English language? I would choose to believe it was man's error before I would believe that God lied and confused us, and with this belief, I am not the least bit confused.

This makes the word of God fit perfectly with everything else we have read in his word. Jesus Christ himself understood God's plan at that very moment on the cross when God revealed it to him. God did not forsake his Son any more than he would forsake us. Also remember Jesus said, "All these things that I do and greater things can ye do also, because I go unto the Father." God could not reveal this before that time because if Satan had figured it out, he (Satan) would not have crucified Jesus. Remember, none of the princes of this world knew, for had they known, they would not have crucified the Lord of Glory. Satan would have known of the greater things, and his job would be much easier if Jesus was the only one walking around able to do the works he did—much less the greater things (the manifestations) we can all now do if we chose to. Now the word of God fits together with mathematical exactness, with God's plan and purpose and with no contradictions.

Could we have been given a clue that we should study this? There had to be an error somewhere because God does not lie and he said,

"I will never leave thee nor forsake thee." This is why God's word tells us in 2 Timothy 2:15, "study to shew thyself approved unto God, a workman that needeth not to be ashamed, rightly dividing the word of truth." We are also told to search the scriptures, and to meditate upon these things, and be doers of the word and not hearers only. God knew that man would be involved in the translations. We could not have read them in Greek or Hebrew or Aramaic. Studying and being a doer is how we hide God's word in our heart with understanding. How else can you make it your own and live by every word?

Like the Bible, so many things have happened in my life that document God's word, one book cannot contain it all. So I will leave you with these thoughts. When I came to God's word and formed a personal relationship with him as a true Father, I searched him and his word daily with such excitement for what I had found. I could see the exactness of his word, correcting the imperfections I had in my life with scientific precision. Like the tithe, the more time I gave to God and his word, the more time I had. Everything I had to do was done with time to spare. I could not out-give God, even the night I searched his word until 4:00 a.m. I fell asleep at the wheel driving on the highway with the cruise set at 72 mph. An angel woke me with one soft word, "Carrie." As I opened my eyes, I saw at a glance that a man in the passenger seat was driving my car with his left hand.

As I took hold of the steering wheel and looked back, he was gone. I thought about this the rest of the drive home, and realized how personal God is. It was my biological father's voice when I heard my name. He woke me like when I was a child so I wouldn't be startled.

If you think you don't have time to read, study and search God, because of your to-do list, remember this: the Bible says that God knows your need. He will fill it, even better than you can, and you cannot out-give him.

Eleven years later, I have this same excitement, with examples to share with you that God's word is true and personal. He designed it to cater to your personal needs. Whatever church you go to, you don't have to leave God and his word there. God wants to be a member of every family and home. This is why he equipped each of us with himself, his Son and the angels. As I said before, if God expected us to be perfect on our own, we wouldn't need them.

There is no limit to our understanding of the world when God himself is the one that gives it. Through the Spirit in us that only comes from knowing who his Son is, we have a wisdom available that man cannot teach us. This is the difference between the natural man that receives not the things of the Spirit, and the spirit man that can receive—spirit to spirit, from God through Jesus Christ the mediator—like a connection cable that reconnected us with God.

This book has only touched the surface of what God and his word can do in your life. If you choose to bring your every thought to his word he will direct your path, showing you with signs, miracles and wonders. Each and every day he will shower you with blessings. When you need an angel, he will send one, even if it's just to get you back on track. So let the desires of your heart be known to God. Talk to him; he will listen and respond.

Anytime you find you want or need more remember, God will give to you what you ask and believe for. Satan will give you the negatives you confess.

As I said on the back cover of this book, I do not have the answers, but God does. If you choose to continue seeking your answers from God, not just any man or book, being able to recognize any contradictions to his word, and bringing your every thought to him and his book, he will direct your path! This is how your answers and your understanding will be unlimited.

> Jeremiah 33:3, "Call unto me, and I will answer thee, and shew thee great and mighty things, which thou knowest not."

> Matthew 7:8, "For every one that asketh receiveth; and he that seeketh findeth; and to him that knocketh it shall be opened."

And may God bless you all!
Love
Carrie
Your sister in Christ